My Father's Story:
The Murder of the Best Man I've Ever Known

Eric Johnson

Copyright © 2023

All Rights Reserved

ISBN: 978-1-961804-29-6

Dedication

To my father and best friend, William Joseph Johnson. Love you, Pops!

Acknowledgment

I would like to thank: my family, friends, and my father's friends for their unwavering support and love during these past few years. To the prosecutor, for doing an amazing job presenting the case. To the Michigan State Troopers, Forensic Scientists, and medical examiner who worked on his case, thank you for your professionalism and attention to detail.

The names and locations referenced in this book (from the court hearings) have been changed or redacted to protect and give some anonymity to those involved.

About the Author

Eric Johnson is a security professional from Michigan. Eric graduated with high honors from Madonna University and holds over 20 professional certifications. He has worked in asset protection, several security command centers, and as an emergency manager and business continuity advisor for a large mortgage company. Eric also teaches special guest lectures at colleges several times a year. Outside of his career, he is a devoted family man and friend. With a zest for life, he enjoys: working on cars, going on road trips, writing and playing music, concerts, watching movies and podcasts, and is an avid foodie.

Contents

Dedication iii

Acknowledgment iv

About the Author v

Chapter 1: The Man, The Father, The Legend 1

Chapter 2: Falling for the Wrong One 8

Chapter 3: The Unthinkable Tragedy 16

Chapter 4: The Beginning 23

Chapter 5: Final Status Conference 34

Chapter 6: The Start 40

Chapter 7: Eleven 55

Chapter 8: Grandfather 68

Chapter 9: Firefighter 76

Chapter 10: EMT 1 90

Chapter 11: EMT 2 98

Chapter 12: Trooper 1 111

Chapter 13: Trooper 2 124

Chapter 14: Trooper 3 143

Chapter 15: Forensic Scientist 1 153

Chapter 16: Forensic Scientist 2 167

Chapter 17: Trooper 4 176

Chapter 18: Detective Trooper 1 190

Chapter 19: Trooper 5 223

Chapter 20: Detective Sergeant 1 231

Chapter 21: Detective Sergeant 2 242

Chapter 22: The Aftermath of Day 1 263

Chapter 23: Funeral Home Director 267

Chapter 24: Medical Examiner 1 272

Chapter 25: Forensic Psychologist 1 300

Chapter 26: Forensic Psychologist 2 323

Chapter 27: The Court's Ruling 337

Chapter 28: What Now? 355

MY FATHER'S STORY

Chapter 1: The Man, The Father, The Legend

"A father is the one friend upon whom we can always rely. In the hour of need, when all else fails, we remember him upon whose knees we sat when children, and who soothed our sorrows; and even though he may be unable to assist us, his mere presence serves to comfort and strengthen us."

-Émile Gaboriau

These words from Émile Gaboriau ring true for many of us. Fathers are often seen as the authority figure in a family, but they also play a vital role in building emotional connections and creating happy memories. From teaching their children to catch their first fish to helping them with school, moving them, and providing guidance during tough times, fathers make a tremendous impact.

A father may not always know the right thing to say or do, but his willingness to try and be present for his children is what counts. He is blessed with the power to shape his children's lives by modeling positive behaviors and instilling important values such as kindness, respect, and responsibility.

Although every father has his own way of parenting, one thing is certain - the love and support he provides can make all the difference in his child's life.

ERIC JOHNSON

I was fortunate enough to have a father who not only fulfilled his role as a dad but also became one of my closest confidants. I affectionately called him *Pops*, and we would communicate through text or phone calls every other day.

During our phone conversations, I found myself laughing more than any other time in my day. This was due to my father's ability to make every conversation funny and engaging. Whenever we answered each other's calls, we would shout *WAZZUP!* like in the movie *Scary Movie* or the famous beer commercial.

One of the aspects I valued most about my dad was his ability to talk about literally anything. We would talk about anything from: music, school, cars, food, movies, motorcycles, dating, guns, drama, the bands I was playing in, and anything we could think of. Nothing was off-limits between us, as we were completely transparent with each other. Despite not always seeing eye to eye, my father treated me with the utmost respect. Whenever we disagreed, he would calmly explain his thoughts and remain respectful of my opinions. As I grew older, our relationship evolved from a parent-child dynamic to best friends.

My bond with my dad grew even stronger when I was a teen and I developed a passion for cars. Back in the day, when Pops used to be a mechanic, he was always down to help me and my friends out with our cars.

MY FATHER'S STORY

He was a master of his craft. He started as a mechanic and then became a clerk at a parts store later in life. Being a mechanic was tough work, but you could tell my dad loved it. He loved anything with a motor, and he poured his heart and soul into every job he took on. With over 20 years of experience in the industry, he loved nothing more than passing on his knowledge to friends and family. He was always willing to lend a helping hand, and his work on everyone's vehicles was nothing short of exceptional. Pops was a true professional, and his dedication to his craft was inspiring. He was meticulous in his work, never rushing through a job, and his attention to detail was unmatched. Pops took those traits into every aspect of his life.

I always loved to work on my ride with him and soak up all the knowledge I could. He was a great teacher, super patient, and would break everything down for me in detail. I remember feeling so grateful for his guidance and support. He never made me feel silly for asking questions or making mistakes. Instead, he encouraged me to keep trying and learning from my experiences.

When I turned 16, I was gifted a 1996 Chevy Malibu by my mom and stepdad. Pops and I couldn't wait to start changing out parts! Cause, after all, life is too short to stay stock, right?

We added better speakers, LED lights inside, a hook-up for my phone, and an air intake. Eventually, Pops came up with the wild idea to put an old Harley Davidson muffler on it. Once we heard how deep and loud it sounded, we knew it was a game-changer. It added a whole new level of personality to my car and made it stand out from the rest. It would set off some car alarms, and my mom could even hear me coming from down the street!

I loved hearing about Pop's job, especially when he started working at an auto parts store in Manistee, MI. He'd tell me about these wild Frankenstein Machines people would bring in and ask him to find parts for. He also had such a love for his coworkers. They were his best friends up there, and I can see why, as they have become my friends now.

During the time Dad lived in Dearborn Heights, we created countless unforgettable memories. It's difficult to choose just one favorite moment! We enjoyed a variety of activities, such as: attending concerts, cruising around on his 100th-year special anniversary Harley Davidson, attending car shows, motorcycle shows, monster truck shows, gun and knife shows, fishing on his boat, hanging with his friends or mine, and exploring art and street festivals. It felt like we were always on the go, busy doing something exciting. But what made these experiences truly special was the time we spent together as father and son.

When I was younger, Pops owned a small cottage up north, right on the water. It was a place where we could escape the hustle and bustle of everyday life. We spent countless hours working on the cottage and enjoying the beautiful surroundings. Looking back, some of my most cherished memories with him were made during those trips up north.

MY FATHER'S STORY

Later in his life, Pops achieved one of his dreams. He bought a property up north on 10 acres of land with a beautiful house and pole barn. My father's property was a true oasis, nestled deep in the Manistee National Forest; it did not even have Wi-Fi! After Pops moved up north, hiking became one of our favorite activities. We would explore his property and take in the breathtaking scenery. Another favorite pastime was taking walks with Xena—oh wait! I haven't introduced Xena!

Well, Xena was my father's beloved 130-pound Cane Corso dog. Xena was a loyal companion who accompanied Pops on exploring his property.

Whenever I visited Pops, Xena would come running over to me with unbridled joy. She would bark excitedly to let my dad know I had arrived. He spoiled her rotten, making sure to include her in our Sunday morning breakfast ritual of scrambled eggs and toast with peanut butter. Xena would get her own eggs and peanut butter toast. She would finish hers, then sit patiently at the end of the table, waiting for any scraps we were willing to share.

He was also an excellent dog trainer and taught her how to sit, lay down, stay, come, and even shake hands. But the most adorable trick he taught her was how to speak. Yes, Xena would actually answer you if you talked to her. My dad would hold up a piece of peanut butter toast and ask her to say, "I love you." To our amazement, she actually figured out how to bark back, making a sound close to those three words.

Pops and Xena would sit in the house and watch the wild animals come to eat. Whenever Xena would bark at them, Dad would remind her to be nice to the furry neighbors. She loved to chase after the deer, squirrels, and rabbits that came to visit. While Xena had a big heart and just wanted to play, she was never actually able to catch up to the furry neighbors.

Pops would feed the animals around his house every single day, without fail. He'd make sure they had breakfast and dinner every morning and night. He even went the extra mile and built a wooden trough right at the edge of the woods on his property so they could chow down in peace. During his first winter living up north, it rained and snowed so much that the poor animals' food got all soggy. Pops felt terrible for them, so he even built a small roof over the trough to keep their food dry.

When I would come to visit him, we would go downtown Manistee, where we would drive by the beach and take in the beautiful view. Then, we would head to North Channel Brewing Company to enjoy a flight of beer and food. Other times, we would have bonfires, hike through the property with Xena, do some woodworking, work on the cars, clean up the yard, grill some steaks, and relax the evening away watching movies. My dad loved a good movie, with some of his favorite series; *Fast and the Furious series, The Punisher, Terminator,* and other action-packed films. I would download the latest movies on my computer at my apartment, and then we would plug it into his TV to watch them with a cold beer or Angry Balls (a drink made of Angry Orchard hard cider and Fireball whiskey mixed together).

Pops had his own sense of humor that never failed to keep us in stitches. I remember one time when we were watching a horror movie together, and one of the main characters picked up a small boat motor, started it, and used it as a weapon. My dad yelled, "What does that boat motor run on? Hopes and dreams?!"

I know as you are reading this, you might think it's not funny, but the way he said it at that moment, I was rolling on the floor! Looking back on those days, I realize how fortunate I was to have those moments and experiences with my father.

As I reflect on my relationship with my father, I am reminded of the quote I mentioned by Émile Gaboriau at the beginning of this chapter. The mere thought of his presence gives me comfort and strength. While at his funeral, I couldn't help but take in all the people commenting about how great Pops was. Almost everyone said to me, "He was one of the best men I've ever known." Well, I couldn't agree more. I can only hope to be as great of a man as he was.

So as the kids say… This is where the shit gets real. Now is the time to stretch, get a drink. Maybe even make one of Pop's favorites—Angry Balls—because we are about to lay the backstory for this wild ride.

Chapter 2: Falling for the Wrong One

Welcome back, friends! So, let's dive in!

Love - the emotion that makes us blind often forces us to do bizarre things. As the great William Shakespeare said, "Love is blind and lovers cannot see the pretty follies that themselves commit". But oh, how sweet it is to be lost in its intoxicating embrace. We feel like we want to dive head first, despite knowing it has captivated and broken the hearts of countless people throughout history.

Love is a powerful force that can make us feel alive and complete. It teaches us patience, forgiveness, and empathy. It makes us more compassionate and understanding toward others. It can also be a double-edged sword, bringing both joy and pain. When we are in love, we often overlook the flaws and imperfections of our partners and sometimes even ignore red flags that should have been warning signs. We become so consumed by our emotions that we lose sight of reality.

Honestly speaking, I don't have anything against love. It's just that my perspective on things, especially love, has shifted since my dad's murder. You see, the woman who brought my dad so much joy and love ended up being the reason for his death. Ironic, isn't it?

MY FATHER'S STORY

It's hard for me to believe that love won't bring pain and heartache, especially when I've seen firsthand how it can destroy someone's life. But at the same time, I know that my dad wouldn't want me to close myself off from love completely. So, I think it's better to say that I'm just trying to find a balance between being cautious and open-minded when it comes to love. It's a journey, but I know that with time and healing, I'll be able to fully embrace love again.

Now, let me introduce you to the villain of the story: Angelee Ross.

It was 2014 when Angelee had started her new job at the auto shop Pops worked at. Dad was a master mechanic, and Angelee was a service advisor. I remember the days when I would bring Pops lunch between my college classes, and Angelee would join us. She was always kind and inclusive, asking about my life and interests.

As time passed, I began to notice changes in her behavior. Angelee's demeanor had shifted, and she started acting like a high school girl who had a huge crush on my dad. She would get giddy and have trouble looking at my dad. It was obvious to me that she had fallen for him; I was young but not stupid. When I told my dad, we both had a good laugh. Little did we know, this was just the beginning of their story.

As the weeks went by, Angelee's crush on my dad only seemed to intensify. She would find excuses to be around him and would blush whenever he spoke to her. It was almost like watching a teenage girl with a celebrity crush.

Over the next few months, Angelee became a regular at Pop's house. We would laugh, joke, and do fun things together. It was clear that my dad and Angelee had a special connection. And then, one day, my dad took me out to dinner and told me the news - he and Angelee were now a couple. I was happy for them both.

During the initial days of their relationship, Angelee was super considerate and thoughtful. I remember one time she looked at me and said,

"Eric, I'm not here to steal your dad away from you. If you ever feel like I'm getting in the way, just let me know. I want to make sure you have lots of one-on-one time with your dad still."

She sounded so sincere, and it made me feel a lot better about the whole situation. Plus, she was always nice to me from the get-go, so I trusted her. Even my dad couldn't see any flaws in her, but that's what happens when you're in the honeymoon phase of a relationship; everything seems perfect and flawless.

Whenever I visited them, we would have food together. She would ask me all about what was going on in my life. I never once doubted her intentions because she made my dad so happy, and that was all that mattered to me.

MY FATHER'S STORY

Angelee had 2 teenage boys from a previous relationship. She thought I would be a positive influence on them and help motivate them as they were both very reclusive and didn't have direction.

Angelee had seen how I interacted with her, my friends, and people in general, and she believed that my outgoing personality and positive attitude could rub off on her sons. She hoped that I could help them find their way in life. I was in my early twenties at the time; I knew that teenage years were tough, especially when you feel lost or unsure of yourself.

It was not very long after these conversations that she and her sons moved in with my dad. At this time, my dad resided in a small 3-bedroom house in Dearborn Heights, MI. Her sons would rarely come out of their rooms. They would spend all day in their room playing video games. When they did come out of their rooms, it was only to eat food and use the restroom. My dad was not used to having two teenage boys who seemed to have no interest in anything other than their video games. He tried to engage them in conversation and encourage them to participate in family activities, but they were always reluctant and uninterested.

It was then that Pops and Angelee adopted Xena, who was an adorable baby at the time, and her 130-pound grandmother Storm. Storm was just as amazing a dog as Xena! Storm would walk up to you, sit next to you, and set her paw on you to get your attention to give her love. She loved taking care of Xena and keeping her in line. If Xena was getting in trouble, Storm would use her paw and hold Xena down until she stopped her shenanigans. Despite their size difference, Xena and Storm were the best of friends. They would often play together in the backyard or cuddle up next to each other on the couch. Pops and Angelee couldn't have been happier with their decision to adopt both dogs.

However, in 2016, after several years of dating, my father gave me a call to tell me that he and Angelee had decided to break up. Everything had settled peacefully, and there was no drama. My father assured me that they were still friends. Yet he didn't reveal why they broke up. It was decided that Angelee and her kids were going to continue to stay at the house for some time while they figured out where to eventually move. Angelee, Dad, and I would still have dinners together and hang out as if they were just back to being friends.

After about a year of separation, my father and Angelee got back together around the time when one of their dogs, Storm, passed away. It was toward the end of the same year, 2017, when my father bought his dream home up in the Manistee National Forest I told you about previously. Pops, Angelee, and her youngest son moved up there in September. Her oldest son would eventually move up there after dropping out of tech school.

MY FATHER'S STORY

I would go visit Pops as often as I could! Dad, Angelee, and I had many great times, and I always loved going up for visits. Around two years passed on like this until I visited my dad in November of 2019. I went for a weekend to celebrate my birthday with my dad. We went out to dinner, and as I talked to him, he revealed that he and Angelee had broken up once again, and this time on bad terms.

Angelee claimed he was not good at communicating his emotions. She also didn't like he was upset that her kids were not helping around the house, not looking for jobs, not going to school, or even helping with Xena.

I asked, "Pops, what do you mean they are not helping around the house?"

Dad went on to explain how the kids would only leave their rooms to make food and use the bathroom. When they would make food, they would leave a mess all over the kitchen. And when Angelee would ask them to clear up the mess, they would just refuse so either Dad or herself would clear it up. They would even eat food and drinks he was planning to take for lunch at work. My dad went so far as to write his name on the food and drinks that he bought for work. Despite that, her kids would still eat/drink them. Both her kids especially hated helping with yard work and did as little as possible.

I then asked my dad, "They won't help with Xena?"

He explained how only her kids were home during the day since he and Angelee worked. Xena would bark and beg to go outside, but they wouldn't stop playing video games or come out of their rooms to let her out. Xena would then pee in the corner of my dad's bedroom, and he would have to clean it up later. Sometimes Xena would drink all of her water during the day. Her kids would not stop playing video games or come out of their rooms to get her more. Even if they did come out of their rooms to eat or use the bathroom, they still wouldn't let Xena out or check on her water.

I then asked if she and the kids were going to keep living in the house. He replied no and said, "They were moving out soon."

Angelee and her kids moved out for about 2 months in early 2020. Their situation didn't work out, so my dad was gracious enough to allow them to move back in. During this time, Angelee was not employed, and neither were her kids, but they received government aid which did not cover their bills. My father was incredibly generous and offered to help them pay their car insurance and cell phone bills. And unfortunately, at the same time, Angelee's truck engine died. My father even gave her a loan to get a new engine and repair the truck.

In the early summer of 2020, she and her kids moved out to an apartment in Cadillac, MI, that was 30 minutes away from my dad's house. He even paid several months of her rent to help her. She eventually came to realize my dad was right about her kids not being helpful around the house and mistreating Xena. As soon as she realized it, she apologized to my dad. They became friends again and would do dinner on occasion, or she would occasionally come walking or hiking through my dad's property with Xena.

Around Christmas 2020, Pops mentioned to me that Angelee was stressed because she still didn't have a job, and her sons were not helping her. She also had anxiety because of what was going on in the world around us, with the pandemic and political climate in the US. From then until March 15th, 2021, the last time I talked to my dad on the phone, he kept telling me those same things about her. I could tell in his voice; he was never that worried, though. Many people around that time were having the same fears! Although, as we know now… Pops should have been very worried.

Chapter 3: The Unthinkable Tragedy

It was Wednesday, March 17th, 2021. The day began normally, and everything was as usual. I woke up and got ready for work. At this time, I was working as an Asset Protection Team Leader for a retail chain. While listening to my favorite band, *Intervals,* I drove from my apartment to my home store. I walked in and went right to the Starbucks to grab a cold brew coffee. I then went for my usual walk around the store to check for security issues, greeting my fellow leaders and employees as I saw them.

I finally made it to my office and saw I had an online training to attend from 11 a.m. to 1 p.m. I remember how eager I was for the training to end so I could get some lunch, and when the training finished right at 1 p.m., I stood up from my desk to have a stretch. My cell phone was sitting on my desk when it flashed on and caught my eye, I immediately grabbed it, and I saw I had a Facebook message at 1:02 p.m. When I opened it, it was from my dad's boss and one of his best friends, Brad.

The text said, "Can you call me?" with a cell phone number.

I thought to myself, *Great... Dad did too much work and hurt himself.* So, I dialed Brad's phone number, and he answered right away.

MY FATHER'S STORY

"What's going on, Brad?" I asked him.

He said, "Have you spoken to Michigan State Police yet?"

I said no, and he continued, "I'm so sorry to be the one to tell you this, but your father was murdered by Angelee."

I felt my heart drop to my stomach as I tried to process what Brad had just told me. My mind was racing with questions and disbelief. Brad went on to say that my dad was supposed to be the first one at the auto parts store to open it at 8 a.m. When he got there at 8:30 a.m., Pops wasn't there!

Brad instantly knew something was really wrong as my dad never missed a day at work, let alone not show up without telling him. He immediately dialed 911 and asked them to do a welfare check at my dad's place.

The dispatcher took a second and replied, "I'm sorry, Brad, but there is already an active crime scene at this address." He hung up the phone and began speeding toward my dad's house. He told me that when he reached Pop's house, Michigan State Police had yellow taped off the house: "Caution, Crime Scene, Do not cross."

The police officer greeted Brad at my dad's place and interviewed him right there, asking questions like what he knew about Pop and Angelee. He told the officer about the strange episode with Angelee that happened the day before.

Angelee showed up at my dad's auto parts shop but remained in the car and called at store, asking my dad to meet her in the parking lot. After talking with her for several minutes, my dad returned to the store, and she left.

Brad asked, "What was that about?" to my father. Pops said that Angelee was making bizarre comments regarding the horror film series *The Purge* being real, and she wanted him to leave work cause it was not safe. A little while later, Angelee called the shop again and asked to speak with my dad. She went on to tell my dad that she was at his house and the power was out, so he needed to leave work and come take care of Xena.

My dad thought that Xena would be okay for a few hours until he would return home soon to take care of the power. Brad and my dad visited the power company's website right away and saw that his home was the only one without electricity.

The officer thanked him for his statement and let him go. So, he immediately messaged me on Facebook, asking me to call back.

Brad continued by saying that he and Pops were the last to leave work that day. He stopped Pops in the parking lot and said, "Why don't you get Xena and come stay the night with me and my family? I really don't like this weird stuff Angelee is saying." My dad replied to him, "Thanks, but don't worry! I know she is saying weird stuff, but she will

MY FATHER'S STORY

be fine, and I'm going to try to get her help." Brad and Pops got in their separate trucks and left.

As soon as Brad finished telling the story, I felt lost. I just remember asking him if Michigan State Police had her in custody and to which he replied they did. "Keep me updated if you hear any other news because I need to make phone calls," I said and hung up the phone.

My heart started aching more than I can put into words. I was crying, pacing back and forth, not knowing what to do. It was hard to imagine my life without my father and best friend, and the pain kept raging at me. Yet I mustered my strength and called my uncle, my father's brother.

"Hello there, Nephew!" he greeted right away in his characteristically upbeat voice.

I said, "Uncle, I need you to sit down." He promptly responded that he already was.

"Angelee killed Pops. He is dead, and she is in custody."

My uncle could only say "Oh no" on repeat after hearing this over the phone. I told him that I needed to call my mother and that I would call him back if I got any further news.

I called my mother.

"Hey, buddy!" she said in her typically upbeat voice, "What is happening?" I told her the same thing I told my uncle.

She couldn't believe it and said, "I'm coming to get you. Are you at your home store?"

I responded, "Yes, in my office," and she hung up the phone. At this time, I was so overtaken by emotions that I slid down the wall I was standing by and sat on the floor sobbing. I couldn't put into words the storm of emotions that was brewing in my body.

I called one of my best buddies so that he could tell our group of coworkers/friends. After that, I called my boss, who had been in a meeting. She texted back, "Can I call you later? Everything okay?" I responded with, "No, I'm not okay. My dad was just murdered."

She called me right away, and I was crying so hard that she might not have understood a word I said. My boss made sure I had someone coming to get me, to which I responded yes, and I hung up the phone. I then took my work phone and called the leader in charge of my home store.

She answered super cheery but could immediately tell I was sobbing. I hardly managed to tell her that I was leaving work because my dad had just been murdered when she asked what was wrong. While we waited for my mother and stepfather to come, she asked if I was in my office and came running to sit with me. Our HR representative joined us too.

When my mom and stepdad arrived, they rushed into my office, and we all began to sob together. My mom took me to my apartment to get some clothes, and then we headed toward my mom and stepdad's house. The 40-minute drive between my apartment and my mom and stepdad's house was a complete blur.

A Michigan State Police Detective called me while we were driving. I'm not even sure what I said to him, but I do recall telling him that I knew why he had called. He expressed his condolences and asked if he could ask me some questions.

While I don't remember all the questions he asked, I can still recall asking him about Xena after we had gone through several questions. He paused and sighed but finally said, "I'm so sorry, but she killed both of the dogs…" I began crying again and explained which dog was Xena and that the other dog was hers. We eventually got to my mom and stepdad's house. I remember calling several of my friends and my dad's friends to break the news to them.

With every phone call I made to each of his friends, I began to cry more and more. One of my closest friends, known as the Old Man, and my uncle (the one previously mentioned) came over. We were all still in shock. We talked about the funeral, whether we could discover any information on his murder online, to what Brad and the Michigan State Police Officer had talked about with me, but nothing could console us.

The weight of Pop's absence was suffocating, all-consuming, and the thought of living without him felt like the most scary feeling I had ever felt. And to make matters worse, his death was not a natural one. It was a brutal murder by someone he once loved.

Chapter 4: The Beginning

Let's just be honest... Mondays are the worst day of the week. We all dread waking up, getting ready, going to the office, or logging into that computer from home and starting that work week. We have a whole 5 days of hard work, countless meetings, struggles, things going wrong, dealing with that awful coworker we all hate, and being exhausted until the weekend again... Mondays are just the worst. Well, let me tell you, Monday, September 20th, 2021 was one of those legendary bad Mondays.

It had been over six months since Pops and Xena were murdered, and it was time to start the court case against their killer. Yes, what they say about the wheels of justice moving slowly is very true. Even slower than you move the next morning after drinking a dozen Angry Balls and eating too many tacos the night before.

While the Prosecutor and lead Michigan State Police Detective in the case were amazing in communicating with me. They even met with me prior to the court date to let me ask questions, but there were many questions they could not answer. Pop's murder was still considered an open case; they could only tell me so much before the trial. One of the things the prosecutor forewarned me of was that he believed that Angelee and her Defense Council would most likely try to plead "Not Guilty by Reason of Insanity".

This defense, if it was found by the court, would allow Angelee to not serve time in prison but rather serve time in a mental health institution to receive treatment. If she is found "Not Guilty by Reason of Insanity" based on law, she would be entitled to a hearing once a year through probate court to see if she had made enough progress with treatment to be put in a less secure facility or even released back into the public.

After figuring this out, you could only imagine my reaction and the feelings I had inside. She had killed my father, Xena, and even her own dog... the fact that there was even a small chance she could be out in the free world again was beyond enraging. However, I was assured by the prosecutor that not only would several people have to sign off on this but that he was going to do everything in his power to not let that happen. He had planned to make the court record so detailed with how brutal her crimes were that no one would ever consider letting her go after reading them, even if she did make progress with treatment.

It was early in the morning, and my mom arrived at my apartment. We hopped in my car and began the two and half hour drive up to Manistee, MI. The whole drive was filled with tension as we didn't know what to expect and if Angelee would even be in the courtroom. COVID had really messed up the courtroom procedures, and some courts were even doing full procedures via video conferences.

MY FATHER'S STORY

We arrived at the courthouse in Manistee, MI. We had arrived early to make sure we did not miss any of the proceedings. The courthouse is an old building nestled in the middle of a neighborhood, not far from the beautiful downtown area. We made the walk from the parking lot through the front door, where we were greeted by a court officer.

The officer asked us to remove everything from our pockets and walk through the metal detector. As we were removing everything and he was searching my mom's purse for weapons, he asked, "Do you know where you guys are going today?"

I replied that we were not sure where to go and that we were there for the hearing of Angelee Ross. He quickly looked up at me, his eyes got wide, and he said, "Oh, okay. You will need to go down this long hallway, up the elevator to the 3rd floor, and down the long hallway to the very end. The courtroom will be on the right." My mom and I gathered our things and began to head that way.

As we began to walk down the hall, it felt like time stood still. This walk just to the elevator felt just as long as the two and half hour ride we just took. We pressed the up arrow on the elevator. The elevator arrived promptly, and we got in.

As we arrived on the 3rd floor, that feeling of getting sick hit my stomach. You know the one... That awful feeling of nervousness and that something bad is waiting for you. The long walk down the hall felt like it was in slow motion or like Keanu Reeves in *The Matrix*. Everything around me felt like it was moving slowly, but my heart and mind were racing.

We arrived at the end of the hall and were greeted by another court officer. He said, "Good morning. What case are you both here for?"

My mom replied, "Angelee Ross." He said the previous case was still going on and to please take a seat on one of the benches. After waiting for the longest 15 minutes of my life, the people in the previous case exited, and we were allowed to enter.

As I mentioned, COVID really messed up the court system, so the chairs in the gallery where the public could sit were very spread out. Where in normal times, it could have held somewhere around 50 people, there were 15 chairs. My mom and I took seats directly behind the prosecutor's table.

A few minutes went by until several people entered, including the prosecutor. He immediately came up to my mom and me to greet us. He assured us today would be one of the quicker days in court and that Angelee would be appearing via video conference from the jail due to COVID. He pointed to a very large TV mounted on the wall, which had a video on it of a small holding room with no one in it. We all took our seats and patiently waited for the hearing to start.

As we waited, we began to hear noise coming from the TV. An officer brought Angelee in and sat her in the chair in front of the camera. She looked very distant, like her body was present in that chair, but her mind was elsewhere. She stared at the screen, and I just hoped she saw me sitting right behind the prosecutor. It was the first time I had seen her (other than her mug shot) since she had murdered Pops. The feelings were beyond overwhelming inside, but I somehow managed to remain quiet, stoic on the outside.

A few minutes later, "All rise!"

Everyone in the courtroom shot up to their feet. The judge entered and took his seat. "You may be seated."

Judge: This is People of the State of Michigan versus Angelee Noel Ross, file 21-5181-FC. Today is the date and time scheduled for an arraignment on a six-count felony information. We are in a virtual courtroom today. I'm the Judge. I'm in the circuit courtroom in Manistee County. Ma'am, are you Angelee Ross?

Angelee: Yes.

Judge: Please raise your right hand. Do you solemnly swear or affirm that any testimony you give today will be the truth, the whole truth, and nothing but the truth, so help you God?

Angelee: Yes.

Judge: Ms. Ross, your attorney, the Chief Assistant Public Defender, is present here in the courtroom, as is the Manistee County Prosecuting Attorney.

Prosecutor: Thank you. Your Honor, the defendant is before the Court this morning for arraignment on a six-count felony information: Count 1 alleges open murder, that is punishable by life in prison: Count 2 alleges killing or torturing animals, that is a maximum four-year and/or $5,000 fine: Count 3 alleges killing or torturing animals, that is a maximum four-year and/or $5,000 fine: Count 4 is a count of felony firearm, that is a two-year consecutive, and it relates to the crime of murder: Count 5 is a count of felony firearm, that is a maximum consecutive two-year which relates to the crime of killing or torturing animals: And Count 6 is a charge of felony firearm, that is a consecutive two-year relating to the charge of killing or torturing animals in the third degree.

Judge: Thank you, prosecutor. Defense Council, does the defense acknowledge receipt of the felony information?

Defense Council: We do acknowledge receipt, Your Honor, that has been provided to Ms. Ross. At this time, she will enter a plea of not guilty by reason of insanity.

Judge: So she does not demand a further reading of the information?

Defense Council: That is correct, Your Honor.

Judge: And she, at this time, is choosing to plead not guilty by reason of insanity consistent with Michigan Court Rule 6.304. Is that correct?

Defense Council: That is correct, Your Honor.

Judge: Mr. Prosecutor, recognizing that this defendant intends to plead not guilty by reason of insanity, it requires a hearing pursuant to Michigan Court Rule 6.304 to determine a number (of) things including establishing a factual basis as to whether or not these crimes have been committed as alleged, do you agree?

Prosecutor: I do, Your Honor.

Judge: So, how much time do you anticipate needing to present such a case?

Prosecutor: Your Honor, probably a minimum of a day, potentially up to two days of witness testimony.

Judge: Well, what I would propose is there certainly is an interplay between Michigan Court Rule 6.304, the plea of not guilty by reason of insanity Court Rule, and our general plea-taking Court Rule 6.302, but there are some additional findings that are required when a defendant chooses to tender such a plea, and the Court Rule requires in addition that the defendant be advised that if she, in fact, does plead not guilty by reason of insanity she must be committed to the Center for Forensic Psychiatry for up to 60 days for an examination, and if she is determined to be a person requiring treatment or a danger to others by the Department it's very possible that you may seek an order of involuntary commitment in the probate court, is that correct, Mr. Prosecutor?

Prosecutor: Correct, Your Honor.

Judge: What I'm going to do is take her plea of not guilty by reason of insanity under advisement and schedule this for a hearing as required by the Court Rule, and there's a number of moving parts to that Court Rule: First, the State, meaning the prosecutor, will have to establish a factual basis for the crimes this defendant is charged with: The Court will also review any evidence that may be introduced by either side regarding the claim of insanity, and at the conclusion of the hearing I will make findings consistent with Michigan Court Rule 6.302 and 6.304; but, I don't see a point at this point in time today to begin the plea taking that's required under 6.302, do you, Mr. Prosecutor?

Prosecutor: I do not, Your Honor, and I would agree with the Court.

Judge: Defense Council?

Defense Council: I agree with the Court's analysis, Your Honor.

Judge: And she does not have bond available to her currently. Is that correct?

Prosecutor: That's correct.

Defense Council: That's correct.

Judge: Then the plea is taken under advisement, that being this defendant's plea of not guilty by reason of insanity. The Court will schedule this -- we'll start with one full day for the plea taking, so you should anticipate having your witnesses available on that date, Mr. Prosecutor, including any witnesses from the Center for Forensic Psychiatry and/or any stipulations regarding reports generated. So she's been evaluated by the Center only with regards to criminal responsibility?

Prosecutor: There has been a competency evaluation, Your Honor, that took place after the criminal responsibility evaluation.

Judge: While this case was still in district court?

Prosecutor: Correct.

Judge: And the Judge ultimately found her competent to stand trial?

Prosecutor: He did.

Judge: And she's not under a course of medication as recommended and/or ordered by the Center for Forensic Psychiatry you shared with me and counsel you shared with me in chambers, counsel, do you agree, Defense Council?

Defense Council: I do agree, Your Honor. The Center for Forensic Psychology has not prescribed any medications. She is taking an antipsychotic medication that was prescribed by the doctor at the jail.

Judge: So whoever is providing medical service -- medical services to our inmate population, that's who's prescribed it?

Defense Council: That's correct, Your Honor.

Judge: Okay. Well, I'm not going to change the bond at this point in time. She'll continue to be held in the Manistee County Jail without bond to await disposition of these matters. But we will get it scheduled for a one-day hearing, we'll start with one full day with regards to the plea taking: If we need more time, we'll certainly schedule some more time.

Prosecutor: Very good. Thank you, Your Honor.

Defense Council: Thank you, Your Honor.

The clerk yelled again, "All rise! The proceedings for today have concluded."

We all shot out of our seats, and the judge retreated back to his chambers. My mom and I exited the long hallway with the prosecutor following right behind us. The prosecutor was right... they were going for the "Not Guilty by Reason of Insanity" defense. We stayed and spoke with the prosecutor for several minutes, then began to head back to my car.

MY FATHER'S STORY

This whole exchange took a matter of ten minutes at most, but it somehow felt like a lifetime and the blink of an eye all at once. On the drive home, my mom and I talked about every little bit of what was said, the next steps, and how Angelee even looked and acted, but I couldn't tell you a word was said. I had so many thoughts going through my head I couldn't manage to pick out and focus on any of them. The one thing I could recall feeling was that this was the beginning of the fight for justice for my father.

Chapter 5: Final Status Conference

Remember how, at the beginning of the previous chapter, I shared my hatred for Mondays? Like literally, they're the worst day of the week. Well, my opinion still hasn't changed. Monday, April 11th, 2022, turned out to be even more of a legendary bad Monday than the one from the previous chapter.

Well, I didn't have any high expectations for the day. It was time to head back up to Manistee, MI, for another court hearing. This time, I made the trip with my mom and one of my friends.

After making it through the two-and-a-half-hour drive, parking, and making our way up to the courtroom, I still felt as miserable as I did the last time. However, when we got off on the 3rd floor and began walking toward the courtroom, that gut-wrenching feeling in my stomach only worsened. Remember that awful, sinking, twisting feeling we talked about before? Yeah, it was there again – only it was far worse.

We were let into the courtroom. As I waited for the hearing to start, I couldn't help but notice my mom as she was talking with one of the court officers. Rushing over to my friend and me, she grabbed my shoulder and said:

MY FATHER'S STORY

"Eric, she is going to be in the courtroom today." I could only stare back at my mom, unable to utter a single word. The thought of her being in the same room made me feel even more sick.

Several minutes went by and eventually, the Prosecutor and Defense Council entered the courtroom. Then it happened...

Through a door at the side of the courtroom, Angelee was escorted in by a court officer. For a moment, I froze in my spot. She was in the standard prison outfit, and her hair was a mess. Her arms and legs were handcuffed, and it looked like she had put on some weight. As she walked, she continued staring at the floor. When she was led to the defense table, her gaze was fixed on the table in front of her.

I had to fight every nerve in my body to keep myself from charging at her. My mom and friend grabbed me, one on each shoulder. Their grip tightened as they felt me shuddering with fury. All I could do was stand still, just clutching my hands together as hard as I could.

After a minute, Angelee slowly turned around in her chair. She briefly looked at my friend, then my mom, and then she locked eyes with me. At that moment, time seemed to have frozen. While this interaction didn't last for more than fifteen seconds, our gaze was locked. It felt like an eternity before she finally pulled away her gaze.

In that fifteen-second brief interaction, I tried to say those million things buried inside me through my eyes. I tried to communicate the storm that raged inside me. Although I'm not sure how it came across to her, I hope she could feel that pure hatred that I felt toward her. She had taken away my father, my best friend, and not to mention Xena too!

During those fifteen seconds, the world seemed to have disappeared around me. It felt like there was nothing and no one but Angelee and me. I couldn't even feel my mom or friend holding on to me.

Following that eye contact, she had turned back, facing the table with her head bowed. After the most intense fifteen seconds of my life, I sat down, feeling an overwhelming amount of emotions.

My mom and friend still held on to me. After another minute, we heard the familiar "All rise!" Everyone in the courtroom shot up to their feet. The judge entered and took his seat.

"You may be seated." The hearing began.

Clerk: People versus Angelee Ross, file number 21-5181-FC.

Prosecutor: Good morning, Your Honor. The prosecutor on behalf of the People.

Judge: Good morning.

Defense Council: Good morning, Your Honor. The Defense Council appearing on behalf of Ms. Angelee Ross, who is present and seated here to my right.

Judge: Good morning. We're scheduled for a final status conference today. Although there is a jury trial scheduled to begin April 27th, 28th and 29th, it's my understanding, after previously discussing with counsel, that those are the days set aside for an evidentiary hearing regarding the defendant's anticipated not-guilty-by-reason-of-insanity plea, is that correct, Mr. Prosecutor?

Prosecutor: That's correct, Your Honor.

Defense Council: Yes, Your Honor.

Judge: Are your witnesses subpoenaed, Mr. Prosecutor?

Prosecutor: For the evidentiary hearing, yes, Your Honor.

Judge: Ms. Defense Council?

Defense Council: Yes, they are, Your Honor.

Judge: So am I being asked at this time to take this matter off the trial docket as it's currently scheduled and simply use those days for the purpose of the People setting forth evidence that the crimes charged have been committed in response to the Court Rule regarding not-guilty-by-reason-of-insanity pleas?

Prosecutor: Yes, Your Honor.

Defense Council: Yes, Your Honor.

Judge: All right. The Court will take the matter off the trial docket, and the three days set aside, April 27th, 28th and 29th, will be used by the Court to hear evidence presented by the State to support a finding that's required in this instance if the Court is to find Ms. Ross not guilty by reason of insanity (NGRI).

Prosecutor: And the court will be taking the NGRI plea at that time?

Judge: Yes, yes.

Defense Council: Thank you, Your Honor.

Judge: We'll start the hearing by and it's an interplay between the NGRI Court Rule and 6.302, but they're melded together. Obviously, it has to be a knowing, understanding, voluntarily plea, but then there also has to be evidence that the crimes charged have been committed, but then also evidence that demonstrates that the defendant was criminally insane at the time, and I assume I'll hear evidence of both?

Prosecutor: Yes, Your Honor.

Defense Council: Yes, Your Honor.

Judge: Okay. Anything further today?

MY FATHER'S STORY

Prosecutor: No, thank you.

Defense Council: No.

Judge: That will conclude today's hearing. Thank you.

The clerk yelled, "All rise! The proceedings for today have concluded."

At the call, we all shot out of our seats, and the judge retreated back to his chambers. For a minute, we stood in the hallway, waiting for the prosecutor to come out. A minute or two later, he approached my mom, my friend, and me. We began talking about the upcoming hearing and what we could expect.

As we stood there talking, I noticed the Defense Council coming out of the room. Approaching our little group, she said, "Pardon me. I'm sorry to interrupt. Are you the son of William Johnson?"

I replied that I was. She said, "I've got to hear a lot about your dad, and I'm so sorry for your loss. He seemed like such an amazing and kind man." She apologized for the interruption again and then left. After concluding our conversation with the prosecutor, we headed toward our car.

The stage was set for April 27th, 28th, and 29th. We would finally hear all the details of what happened and how my dad's killer would spend the rest of her life.

Chapter 6: The Start

This time, the dreaded day was Tuesday, April 26th, 2022. That afternoon, I arrived in Manistee, MI, with my uncle (my dad's brother), mom, stepdad, and one of my friends. Before the hearing, we settled into a hotel and decided to go to North Channel Brewery to grab a beer and have a meal in honor of Pops.

As we ordered our food and drinks, the air was heavy with apprehension. None of us knew what we were there for. We all had so many questions about how the next few days would turn out. We were uncertain about what the future had in store for us, but we took comfort in the fact that at least we were together to support each other.

The next morning, we all woke up early. We decided to have coffee and breakfast at the hotel, but I could only bring myself to have cold-brew coffee. My stomach was in knots, and that awful, sinking feeling had returned. On our drive to the court house, I remained on edge.

As we arrived at the courthouse, one of my best friends and family friends met us there. We all greeted each other in the parking lot, and then we began to walk toward the building. After making it up to the third floor, we all took our seats. At the same moment, the prosecutor and lead Michigan State Police Detective walked in. As we were greeting each other, I noticed the prosecutor went running out of the courtroom.

MY FATHER'S STORY

Before the hearing could begin, I also decided to run to the restroom. As I walked out of the courtroom, I noticed the prosecutor bent over, talking to a young girl. This girl was sitting on the ground with her back against the wall, sobbing hard.

I couldn't help but overhear as she mumbled to the prosecutor in between her sobs, "I'm so scared to see her again."

The prosecutor reminded her that she would be locked up in chains. "She wouldn't be able to hurt you," he told her, trying to calm her down. The young girl's family was bent down as well, trying to comfort her.

Returning to the courtroom, I found my seat right behind the prosecutor. Within a few minutes, the familiar voice of the clerk rang out, "All rise!"

The judge entered the courtroom and sat down.

Clerk: People versus Angelee ROSS, file number 21-5181-FC.

Judge: Good Morning, Mr. Prosecutor.

Prosecutor: Good Morning, Your Honor.

Judge: Good Morning, Ms. Defense Council.

Defense Council: Good Morning, Your Honor.

Judge: Ms. Ross, today's hearing is scheduled at councils' request as an evidentiary hearing regarding an anticipated plea being made by the defendant of not guilty by reason of insanity. Is that correct, Mr. Prosecutor?

Prosecutor: That's correct, Your Honor.

Defense Council: It is, Your Honor.

Judge: So she intends to change her previous not-guilty pleas to the charges she currently faces to not guilty by reason of insanity?

Defense Council: This is correct, Your Honor.

Judge: And the court recognizes that, when looking to the felony information, the defendant is currently charged with six counts by the State of Michigan: count 1 charges the defendant with open murder, which is a felony punishable by up to life in prison: count 2 charges the defendant with animal cruelty in the third degree, a felony punishable by up to four years in prison: count 3 charges animal cruelty in the third degree, also a felony punishable by up to four years in prison: counts 4, 5 and 6 each charge felony firearm which is a felony in Michigan punishable by up to two years in prison, however, if convicted it requires a consecutive sentence which means the two years are served before serving any other sentence imposed, and again, Ms. Defense Council, the defendant intends to change her pleas from not guilty to not guilty by reason of Insanity to all six counts?

Defense Council: Yes, Your Honor.

Judge: Ms. Ross, do your best to raise your right hand. Do you solemnly swear or affirm that (the) testimony you give today will be the truth, the whole truth, and nothing but the truth, so help you God?

Angelee: I do.

Judge: Thank you. Mr. Prosecutor, Ms. Defense Council, do you agree that the court Rules the court shall look to are Michigan Court rule 6.302, which is the general court rule regarding guilty and no contest pleas, but then also Michigan Court rule 6.304 which is our court rule in Michigan that addresses pleas of not guilty by reasons of insanity?

Prosecutor: I do, Your Honor. I believe that 6.304 is to be read in conjunction with the applicable section of 6.302.

Defense Council: And I agree with that, Your Honor.

Judge: Finally, do you agree, Mr. Prosecutor, Ms. Defense Council, that in Michigan, insanity is considered to be affirmative defense as set forth by MCL 768.21a and that Ms. Ross has properly claimed the affirmative defense of insanity by timely notice?

Prosecutor: I do, Your Honor.

Defense Council: We do, Your Honor.

Judge: And by definition, insanity is an extreme or mental illness, one must be mentally ill before he or she can be found insane; but, the converse is not true, which means one can also be mentally ill but ultimately found to be sane, do you agree, Mr. Prosecutor?

Prosecutor: Yes, that's correct, Your Honor.

Judge: Do you agree, Ms. Defense Council?

Defense Council: Yes.

Judge: All right. Now, Ms. Ross, in this instance, have you heard me read into the record the charges that you currently face in the felony information?

Angelee: Yes.

Judge: And do you understand that if you chose not to change your plea from not guilty to not guilty by reason of insanity, and you went to trial, and you were convicted, the maximum possible sentence that you face is up to life in prison with a consecutive two-year sentence also being required to be imposed as a result of the felony firearm charges, do you understand that?

Angelee: Yes.

Judge: You understand? You need to verbalize your answer.

Angelee: Yes, I understand.

Judge: Thank you. Now, because this hearing requires the court to utilize both 6.302 as well as 6.304, I'm going to explain to you, by pleading guilty, by pleading no contest, or by pleading not guilty by reason of insanity, you are giving up a number of rights that you currently have. Do you understand that?

Angelee: I do understand.

Judge: If this Court... if I accept your not-guilty-by-reason-of-insanity plea you're giving up the following: The right to a trial by jury, the right to be presumed innocent until proven guilty, the right to have the Prosecuting Attorney prove beyond a reasonable doubt that you are guilty, the right to have witnesses against you appear at trial, the right to question witnesses against you, the right to have the court order any witnesses you have for your defense appear at trial, the right to remain silent during your trial, as well as the right to not have your silence be used against you by the state if you chose not to speak: Further, you'd be giving up the right to testify at trial if you chose to, do you understand?

Angelee: I understand.

Judge: In this instance, have any promises been made to you to plead not guilty by reasons of insanity to all six counts?

Angelee: No.

Judge: Do you agree, Mr. Prosecutor?

Prosecutor: I do, Your Honor.

Judge: Do you agree?

Defense Council: No promises, Your Honor.

Judge: Have you been threatened in any way to change your pleas from not guilty to not guilty by reason of insanity?

Angelee: No, your Honor.

Judge: Is it your own choice to change your pleas to not guilty by reason of insanity?

Angelee: Yes, Your Honor.

Judge: Have you had enough time to discuss your case with your attorney Ms. Defense Council, the Public Defender?

Angelee: Yes, Your Honor.

Judge: When you've discussed with Ms. Defense Council the charges that you face and the potential outcomes, have you discussed, if you chose instead simply to proceed to trial, what the Prosecuting Attorney would be required to prove to convict you of the crimes you've been charged with?

Angelee: Yes, Your Honor.

Judge: Have you also discussed with Ms. Defense Council, in addition to the affirmative defense of insanity, if there are any other possible defenses that you could raise if you chose to proceed to trial?

Angelee: Yes, Your Honor.

Judge: Have you had those conversations, Ms. Defense Council?

Defense Council: We have, Your Honor.

Judge: Ms. Ross, have you consumed any alcohol, drugs, or medications that have been prescribed to you during the last 24 hours?

Angelee: Yes, Your Honor, I've taken my meds, Zyprexa and Buspar.

Judge: Would you provide just a brief description as to your understanding as to what the Zyprexa and what the Buspar is intended to treat?

Angelee: The Zyprexa is an antipsychotic, and the Buspar is for anxiety.

Judge: And you've taken your medications as your doctor has prescribed?

Angelee: Yes.

Judge: Have you been able to understand the proceedings in your case thus far?

Angelee: Yes.

Judge: Now, turning to 6.304, do you understand that if, ultimately, following the hearing, I accept you're not guilty by reasons of insanity pleas to all six counts, Michigan law requires that I commit you to the center for the Forensic Psychiatry for up to 60 days, do you understand?

Angelee: I understand that.

Judge: And do you also understand that at the conclusion of your stay at the center, the center for Forensic Psychiatry will author a report, and that report will be forwarded to me, and we'll have another hearing, and that report may recommend that I direct the Prosecuting Attorney to proceed in the probate court and seek to have you involuntarily committed as a legally incapacitated person, do you understand?

Angelee: I understand.

Judge: And if that were to occur, you should understand that there is the potential that the result may be hospitalization for up to the rest of your life, do you understand that?

Angelee: I understand.

Judge: Do you agree with the court's statement Mr. Prosecutor?

Prosecutor: I do, Your Honor.

Judge: Do you as well, Ms. Defense Council?

Defense Council: I do, Your Honor.

Judge: Now, we're at the point in the hearing where I'm going to ask you how you plead to the specific charges, Ms. Ross. How do you plead to the charge of open murder, not guilty or not guilty by reason of insanity?

Angelee: Not guilty by reasons of insanity.

Judge: How do you plead to count 2, animal cruelty in the third degree, not guilty or not guilty by reason of insanity?

Angelee: Not guilty by reasons of insanity.

Judge: How do you plead to count 3, animal cruelty in the third degree, not guilty or not guilty by reason of insanity?

Angelee: Not guilty by reasons of insanity.

Judge: How do you plead to Count 4, felony firearm, not guilty or not guilty by reason of insanity?

Angelee: Not guilty by reasons of insanity.

Judge: How do you plead to Count 5, felony firearm, not guilty or not guilty by reason of insanity?

Angelee: Not guilty by reasons of insanity.

Judge: How do you plead to Count 6, felony firearm, not guilty or not guilty by reason of insanity?

Angelee: Not guilty by reasons of insanity.

Judge: Mr. Prosecutor, Ms. Defense Council, we're at the point in time where the court will receive evidence that demonstrates a factual basis for determining whether or not to accept the defendant's not-guilty-by-reason-of-insanity pleas to all six counts, and my interpretation of the court Rule allows evidence frankly to be submitted by both parties, do you agree?

Prosecutor: I do agree with that, Your Honor.

Judge: Do you agree?

Defense Council: Yes, Your Honor.

Judge: The Court is required to find that this defendant has committed the acts as charged, and that's the purpose for the evidentiary hearing: And also, this court is required to find by a preponderance of the evidence that the defendant was legally insane at the time of the offense, and part of the requirement is that the court, I expect, will be provided and review reports generated by the center for

Forensic Psychiatry relative to criminal responsibility as well as any independent evaluations, and I'm aware that we may have not only a doctor from the center for Forensic Psychiatry rendering an opinion that Ms. Ross was not criminally responsible at the time that these crimes were committed as a reason by reason of insanity, but also an independent evaluator. Is that correct, Mr. Prosecutor?

Prosecutor: It is.

Judge: And the independent evaluator was secured by which side?

Prosecutor: That was secured by the People, Your Honor.

Judge: And that doctor supports the center's doctor's conclusion?

Prosecutor: That doctor does.

Judge: All right. Then is there anything further that needs to be addressed by the way of 6.302 or 6.304 before we begin the evidentiary portion of the hearing?

Prosecutor: I don't believe so, Your Honor.

Defense Council: No, Your Honor.

Judge: Mr. Prosecutor, do you care to make your opening statement?

Prosecutor: Your Honor, just that as this is a plea proceeding, I will keep it brief, but I believe that all six counts, after the court is done hearing most of the evidence today and into tomorrow, the court will come away with the firm conclusion that Ms. Ross committed these offenses, that will be based on witness testimony as well as numerous exhibits, photographs and audio recordings. Your Honor, at that point in time, obviously, Ms. Defense Council will present some evidence regarding Ms. Ross' mental state at the time that this occurred: I also believe some of that evidence will come out as the People present witnesses here today. That's all I have. Thank you, Your Honor.

Judge: Ms. Defense Council, do you care to make an opening statement?

Defense Council: Just very briefly, Your Honor. We do agree that the Prosecution's witnesses will establish that these crimes were committed, and obviously, we do plan then to present evidence from Forensic Psychologist 1 from the Forensic Center, and Forensic Psychologist 2, the independent evaluator.

Judge: The final housekeeping matter, last week, counsel approached the court with a binder by stipulation to assist this court in preparing for today's hearing: That binder contained a number of not only police reports but portions of police reports, witness statements, and a portion of a transcribed interview that it's believed was conducted between Detective Sergeant 2 and Ms. Ross, and counsel wanted me to have the.. wanted the court to have the opportunity to review the contents of that binder prior to today's hearing. Is that correct, Mr. Prosecutor?

Prosecutor: That is correct, Your Honor.

Defense Council: Yes, Your Honor.

Judge: And the purpose was to assist the court in preparing for and understanding the testimony that I would be hearing?

Defense Council: Yes, Your Honor.

Prosecutor: That is correct.

Judge: Will that binder be offered into evidence by stipulation as an exhibit because, as you know, at the conclusion (of) the hearing, I'm required to submit a settled record to the Center for Forensic Psychiatry, and having reviewed the contents of that binder I would suggest that it be submitted by way of an exhibit and that can be forwarded as well.

Defense Council: And it will be, Your Honor. It will be submitted as a singular exhibit.

Judge: That's fine.

Prosecutor: Correct.

Judge: And you agree that that will be part of the settled record that I transmit to the Center for Forensic Psychiatry, in addition to transcripts of the hearing that we're going to commence today and hopefully conclude tomorrow, as well as any other exhibits that are received into evidence?

Prosecutor: I agree with that statement.

Defense Council: Yes, Your Honor.

Judge: Okay. Mr. Prosecutor, call your first witness.

Chapter 7: Eleven

Prosecutor: Thank you. Your Honor, I would call Ms. Eleven to the stand.

Judge: Ms. Eleven.

The Clerk: Would you please raise your right hand? Do you solemnly swear or affirm that the testimony you give in this cause will be the truth, the whole truth, and nothing but the truth, so help you God?

Eleven: Yes.

Judge: Ms. Eleven, you can come right in front of the court reporter, and you'll have a seat right next to me, please. Ms. Eleven, this is a large room, and the man in front of me, Mr. Court Reporter, is reporting everything that we say, and it helps him, it helps me, and it helps everyone in attendance if you do your best to speak up nice and loud and clearly, okay?

Eleven: Okay.

Judge: And I know you're soft spoken. If you pull the microphone to you, that will help, I believe. Go ahead, Mr. Prosecutor.

Prosecutor: Ms. Eleven, could you state and spell your name for the record?

ERIC JOHNSON

Eleven: (REDACTED)

Prosecutor: Okay. Great. And where do you live generally in Manistee County?

Eleven: (REDACTED) area.

Prosecutor: Okay. And you're currently in school?

Eleven: Yes.

Prosecutor: And what grade are you in?

Eleven: Eleventh.

Prosecutor: Okay. How old are you, Eleven?

Eleven: Seventeen.

Prosecutor: Okay. I'm going to ask you some questions and everything that I'm going to ask you. I just want the truth here today.

Eleven: Okay.

Prosecutor: Now, I want to ask you about March 17th, 2021, that was around 7:30: Is there something that happened on that date at approximately that time?

Eleven: Yes.

Prosecutor: Okay. Can you kind of take me through what happened?

Eleven: I was going to the post office, and a lady stopped me.

Prosecutor: Okay. Well, let's break that down a little bit. You get up in the morning, and you decide to go to the post office?

Eleven: My mom actually told me to go to the post office to get the mail.

Prosecutor: Okay. To get the mail, so you had a P.O. box there?

Eleven: Yes.

Prosecutor: And this was before school?

Eleven: Yes.

Prosecutor: Okay. And how far away, Eleven, did you live from the post office at the time?

Eleven: About a block.

Prosecutor: And at that time, where were you living?

Eleven: In (REDACTED).

Prosecutor: Okay. And was the post office in (REDACTED) also?

Eleven: Yes.

Prosecutor: Okay. And how do you get to the post office? Did you drive or did you walk?

Eleven: I drove.

Prosecutor: Tell me about that. What happened?

Eleven: I was – like when I drove there?

Prosecutor: Yes.

Eleven: Okay. So like, I drove to the post office and parked and went in to get the mail, and when I came out, the lady was pulling in, and I got in my car, and she blocked me a little bit.

Prosecutor: Okay.

Eleven: So I reversed and like carried on, and she pulled – sorry.

Prosecutor: That's okay. You need a moment?

Eleven: She had the door open as I was reversing and turning around.

Prosecutor: Okay. Let me break that down a little bit. So you said that a woman pulled up behind you?

Eleven: In front of me.

Prosecutor: Okay, and so did that block the passage of your car?

Eleven: It blocked me from getting out, yes.

Prosecutor: Okay. And you said you had reverse to get out?

Eleven: Yeah, because the way that the post office is. The post office parking lot is, you just pull in, and it's a like a little spot in front of the building.

Prosecutor: Okay. And you said that she had the door open: Do you mean the door to your car or the door to her car?

Eleven: The door to her car.

Prosecutor: Okay. And was she in or out of her car at that time?

Eleven: She had her foot out of the car.

Prosecutor: Okay. And do you know what kind of car she was driving?

Eleven: Like a green Suburban like.

Prosecutor: A green Suburban, like a GM type, big?

Eleven: Like a Tahoe, maybe, like something like that.

Prosecutor: An SUV-type vehicle.

Eleven: Yeah.

Prosecutor. Okay. And so you pull out, and what happens then?

Eleven: She shut the door and started following me home.

Prosecutor: And tell me about that. How was she following you?

Eleven: She was just driving really fast behind me, at me.

Prosecutor: Okay. And how close was she to your vehicle?

Eleven: A couple feet.

Prosecutor: Okay. Did it raise your attention someone was driving so close to you? And what happened then?

Eleven: Yeah. I like sped up and got in my driveway, and I was going to like grab my phone, but I couldn't grab my phone, and she came behind me and blocked me in my driveway.

Prosecutor: And what happened after she blocked you in your driveway?

Eleven: She got out of the car and came at my passenger side door.

Prosecutor: And did she get to your passenger side door?

Eleven: Yes, she was like pulling on the handle, asking me if she could get in.

Prosecutor: And she was asking you if she could get in: was the door locked at that point?

Eleven: Yes.

Prosecutor: And did you let her in?

Eleven: No.

Prosecutor: Were your windows up or down at the time?

Eleven: My window was cracked about like half an inch.

Prosecutor: Okay. And did you crack that in order to speak to her?

Eleven: I cracked it because I thought it was my lock button and she was talking because I had to make sure my lock button was closed.

Prosecutor: Okay. And so, do you know how many times she asked you if she could get in?

Eleven: Like five or six times.

Prosecutor: And what was your response?

Eleven: I said no, absolutely not, and then she kept asking me if I was sure.

Prosecutor: Okay. And what happened after she was pulling on your door handle and asking if she could get in? What happened then?

Eleven: I found my phone and grabbed it, and called my mom.

Prosecutor: Okay. And what was the lady doing when you called your mom?

Eleven: She bent over, and I was.. and then as my mom answered – I'm sorry, my mom answered the phone and was asking me what was wrong, and I told her that there was a lady out here trying to get in my car.

Prosecutor: What did the lady do?

Eleven: She just started walking away and got in her car and took off.

Prosecutor: And when she took off, did she have to reverse or did she pull straight out?

Eleven: She just pulled straight out.

Prosecutor: And did she use your driveway or was she on your yard?

Eleven: She drove through my yard.

Prosecutor: And that would be across the lawn?

Eleven: Yes.

Prosecutor: And when you called your mom, was your mom in the house?

Eleven: Yes, she was.

Prosecutor: And did she come out right away?

Eleven: She looked out the window: she didn't believe me that there was a lady trying to get into my car.

Prosecutor: Okay. Now, you've discussed through your testimony here today, Eleven, you've discussed a lady: can you describe the lady?

Eleven: She had blonde hair, blonde curly hair, and she was naked.

Prosecutor: Okay. And when you say she was naked, what do you mean?

Eleven: She had no clothes on.

Prosecutor: Okay. Completely naked? Did she have anything on, do you recall?

Eleven: I don't recall anything exactly, but it looked like she had socks on, like as I looked at her from behind me.

Prosecutor: Okay. But to your recollection, if she had anything on, socks would have been the only thing?

Eleven: What?

Prosecutor: Would socks have been the only thing that she was wearing?

Eleven: Yes.

Prosecutor: Okay. And did you notice anything else about her?

Eleven: Yes. I thought she had like stuff on her, and at first, I thought it was mud, but then it like ringed in that it could have been blood.

Prosecutor: So you saw some things: Where did you see this substance that, at first, you thought it was mud, but then thought maybe it could have been blood?

Eleven: There was some on her face, as I can remember, like a little bit on her face.

Prosecutor: At any point during this interaction, did you, did you ever see (REDACTED) or Grandfather?

Eleven: I seen them pull on the road next to us.

Prosecutor: Okay. And did you see, did you actually see them in their vehicle or did you just see the vehicle?

Eleven: I just seen the car.

Prosecutor: And did you know that the car belonged to (REDACTED)'s Grandfather?

Eleven: Yes.

Prosecutor: Do you know his name?

Eleven: No, he's just papa.

Prosecutor: Okay. And at what point did you see that vehicle?

Eleven: Like after she drove off my.. like after she drove off the road this way onto (REDACTED) I think it is.

Prosecutor: Okay. Well, where were you? Were you still at the post office or were you at home?

Eleven: I was at my house.

Prosecutor: So you could see from your driveway where you were at, you could see (REDACTED)'s grandpa, and you saw the woman drive off?

Eleven: Yes. I can see everything right here, like I can see the whole road or most of the road right here.

Prosecutor: Do you know the crossroads at all?

Eleven: I know the one is (REDACTED), and the one is (REDACTED) or something, I don't remember.

Prosecutor: Okay. And your road at the time, was that a side road off of one of those?

Eleven: Yes.

Prosecutor: Which one was it off of, (REDACTED) or (REDACTED)?

Eleven: The one that the post office is on, so I think (REDACTED).

Prosecutor: Now you said she had blonde hair, was it curly or straight?

Eleven: Curly.

Prosecutor: What size was she, do you know?

Eleven: I can't really recall that.

Judge: Please speak up.

Eleven: I'm sorry. I can't really recall that.

Prosecutor: Okay. And did you notice anything about the way she was acting or the way she spoke?

Eleven: She just seemed a little weird.

Prosecutor: Okay. And what makes you say that?

Eleven: She was just acting weird.

MY FATHER'S STORY

Prosecutor. Okay. Thank you. I don't have anything further.

Defense Council: No questions, Your Honor.

Judge: Thank you, Eleven. You're all set

Chapter 8: Grandfather

Prosecutor: Your Honor, I would like to call Grandfather to the witness stand.

Clerk: Would you please raise your right hand? Do you solemnly swear or affirm that the testimony you give in this cause will be the truth, the whole truth, and nothing but the truth, so help you God?

Grandfather: Yes.

Judge: Mr. Grandfather, if you'd come right around and have a seat next to me, please. Good morning.

Grandfather: Good morning.

Prosecutor: Good morning, Grandfather. Could you please state and spell your name for the record?

Grandfather: (REDACTED).

Prosecutor: And, sir, what do you do for a living?

Grandfather: I'm retired.

Prosecutor: Okay. And where do you live generally?

Grandfather: (REDACTED).

MY FATHER'S STORY

Prosecutor: Okay. Now, I want to ask you about the morning of March 17th, 2021. Were you out and about that morning?

Grandfather: Yes, I was. I picked my grandson and granddaughter up in (REDACTED).

Prosecutor: Okay. Do you know about what time that would have been?

Grandfather: I believe it was just before 7 o'clock in the morning.

Prosecutor: Okay. And you picked them up in (REDACTED), and you went where?

Grandfather: Well, I had to take my granddaughter back to the house so grandma could take her to school, and then I was going to proceed on to .. sorry, (REDACTED) area, drop my grandson off.

Prosecutor: Okay, and?

Grandfather: When I came to the corner of (REDACTED) and .. boy, my mind is just gone.

Prosecutor: That's okay. Take your time if you need.

Grandfather: (REDACTED) and (REDACTED), there's like a three intersection there. I noticed a car sitting on the wrong side of the road where the phone booth used to be back when I was a kid.

Prosecutor: And that's by the school there in (REDACTED)?

Grandfather: Right on (REDACTED), yeah, and I turned down (REDACTED) towards my house and then noticed the car proceeded across (REDACTED) or (REDACTED). I turned on (REDACTED), I believe it is, headed to the house, and I noticed that the car had turned behind me, and I got to the driveway and put the car in park, and turned to tell my granddaughter to have a good day at school, and I noticed a car coming in my driveway, and then I noticed it was coming way too fast and they smacked right into the back of my car and pushed me about a foot and a half, two foot forward.

Prosecutor: Okay. And when you noticed that vehicle was coming way too fast, did you take any precautions? What did you do?

Grandfather: I kept my foot right on the brake. I already had it in park, but I kept it on the brake, I don't know why, but I did. And at impact, I came out of the car unglued, I was ready to kill someone.

Prosecutor: Okay. And what did you see when you got out of the car?

Grandfather: When I went to the front of – I got to the front of her vehicle, the Blazer, and I stopped because I noticed she didn't have no – there was no clothes there. And my wife was coming out of the door at that time, and I told her she needed to deal with this because I didn't believe the lady had any clothes on. She came out, my wife came out and started talking to Angelee and asked her who she was, why she was there, basic questions, and it looked like Angelee was looking through her, you know, like she was spaced. I went in the house and got a one-piece chemical suit and gave it to my wife to give it to Angelee to put on so that she'd have something at least to cover her body. She was covered in blood, and we didn't know any of this, any scenario of - we didn't know. So we treated her as she was a victim at that time. The ambulance came, State Police showed up, they took her to the hospital, and then we took my granddaughter - my wife took my granddaughter to the hospital instead of school.

Prosecutor: Okay.

Grandfather: I had to take my mother to a hearing appointment, and then right after that, I went to the hospital to get checked out.

Prosecutor: Okay. Was everybody that was in your vehicle okay?

Grandfather: Well, no. I received a whiplash and a concussion, and I'm still dealing with it. My granddaughter received some. I think it was a concussion, whiplash, one of those two, because she – think it was more whiplash because she was sitting straight forward. My grandson just... he never did say if he was hurt or not.

Prosecutor: Okay. How old was your granddaughter and grandson at the time?

Grandfather: (REDACTED) is 15.. she was 14, 14, or 15, and (REDACTED) is 18, 19.

Prosecutor: Now you had referred to Angelee, I think is how you referred to the person: would you recognize that person if you saw them again?

Grandfather: I never seen her before in my life. I'm assuming it's this lady right here sitting in front of me.

Prosecutor: Okay. I'm just asking if you would recognize her now if you saw her again.

Grandfather: No.

Prosecutor: How close did you get to her?

Grandfather: To the front of the vehicle.

Prosecutor: Okay. And so, did she ever get out of the vehicle while you were there?

Grandfather: Oh no. I don't think she was capable of walking.

Prosecutor: Okay. And who called the police, was that you or your wife.. or EMS, I should say, not the police.

Grandfather: We called the ambulance. And I'm sure they called the police.

Prosecutor: Okay. And can you describe the vehicle that rear-ended you?

Grandfather: It looked like – like a – kind of like greenish, darker green Trail Blazer.

Prosecutor: Okay. Was it an SUV-type of vehicle?

Grandfather: Yeah, yeah, yeah.

Prosecutor: And what kind of vehicle were you driving that day?

Grandfather: 300 Chrysler.

Prosecutor: And was your vehicle damaged as a result?

Grandfather: Oh yeah. I had.. I think it was like about $3,000 worth of damage to the back of the vehicle.

Prosecutor: And just so we're clear and so the record is clear, the person that rear-ended you in the green SUV, you had never seen that person before?

Grandfather: No.

Prosecutor: And they had no business at your residence?

Grandfather: Not that I know of why she would be there.

ERIC JOHNSON

Prosecutor: Okay. Thank you. I don't have anything further.

Defense Council: Just very briefly, Grandfather, you indicated that you observed Ms. Ross, or at least the woman that rear-ended you in the vehicle: can you describe where she was and what her position was?

Grandfather: She was sitting in the driver's seat. Behind the steering wheel. She was sitting up. As soon as we gave her – she got the chemical suit on, she kind of crouched over and laid down.

Defense Council: She laid down?

Grandfather: Well, laid over into the passenger seat and or onto the console or whatever it was there.

Defense Council: And you described her looking – or looking toward your wife, and you described that it appeared she was looking.. did you say past her or through her?

Grandfather: Through her, like a person spaced out on drugs.

Defense Council: Okay. Thank you. Nothing further.

Prosecutor: I have nothing further from this witness.

MY FATHER'S STORY

Judge: Mr. Grandfather, did you overhear any responses given by this person to your wife when your wife ask who she was and why she was there?

Grandfather: I just heard her say her name was Angelee.

Judge: Thank you, Mr. Grandfather. You're all set. You can go about the rest of your day.

Chapter 9: Firefighter

Prosecutor: Your Honor, I would call Mr. Firefighter to the stand.

Clerk: Would you please raise your right hand? Do you solemnly swear or affirm that the testimony you give in this cause will be the truth, the whole truth, and nothing but the truth, so help you God?

Firefighter: Yes, ma'am.

Judge: Mr. Firefighter, you can come right in front of the bar and have a seat right next to me. Good Morning.

Prosecutor: Mr. Firefighter, could you please state and spell your name for the record?

Firefighter: (REDACTED).

Prosecutor: And Mr. Firefighter, what is your occupation, and for whom do you work?

Firefighter: I do volunteer fire fighting for Maple Grove Fire Department in Kaleva, Michigan, I'm a lieutenant for that, and I also work at the Manistee County Sheriff's Office full-time as a corrections officer.

Prosecutor: Okay. And how long have you been with the Maple Grove Township Fire Department?

MY FATHER'S STORY

Firefighter: Roughly six years.

Prosecutor: Okay. And how long have you been with the Manistee County Sheriff's Department?

Firefighter: About two-and-a-half years.

Prosecutor: Okay. I want to ask you about the morning of March 17th, 2021, at approximately 7:55 a.m. Did anything happen on that day and approximately that time?

Firefighter: We were toned out for a mutual-aid request in (REDACTED) township for a car accident involving.. on.. I can't recall the road, a parked car and another car.

Prosecutor: Okay. And you were working as, just so we're clear, as a Maple Grove Township firefighter at that time.

Firefighter: Yes.

Prosecutor: Okay. And did you proceed to the scene?

Firefighter: Yes.

Prosecutor: Okay. And what did you find when you arrived on the scene?

Firefighter: When we responded to the scene, there were two vehicles, a car and an SUV: The SUV was– behind the vehicle, and there was a –female subject in the vehicle of the SUV.

Prosecutor: Okay. And can you describe the vehicles?

Firefighter: I believe the little car was a Toyota or Chrysler, and then the SUV was a Chevy Tahoe.

Prosecutor: Okay. And do you know what color the Tahoe was?

Firefighter: I cannot recall.

Prosecutor: Okay. Now, what did you do when you arrived on the scene?

Firefighter: When I first arrived on the scene, I walked up with the EMS for MMR, and I noticed that the vehicle was on and the patient's wrist or arm was on the shifter, so I went to the other side of the vehicle to grab the kid, the passenger side, to put in my back pocket so nobody was injured.

Prosecutor: And the vehicle that you're talking about at this point is the Tahoe?

Firefighter: Yes.

Prosecutor: Okay. What happened then?

Firefighter: I proceeded back to the other side of the vehicle to assist MMR with their patient assessment and get information like name, date of birth, and stuff like that.

Prosecutor: Okay. So you had contact with the driver at that point?

Firefighter: Yes, sir.

Prosecutor: What can you tell me about that?

Firefighter: There was a female subject, in and out, who was talking: I was able to get her name and date of birth and have communication with her on that aspect.

Prosecutor: Okay. And when you say in and out, what do you mean?

Firefighter: She was talking, and she was a little confused, which I concerted to a normal car accident. There was dried blood on her face, but that didn't look like it resulted from the accident: there was no airbag deployment or anything.

Prosecutor: Okay. And when you say it didn't look like that blood resulted from the accident, does that have anything to do with the severity of the accident and the amount of blood, or tell me how you came to that conclusion?

Firefighter: The blood was dried, so it looked like it's been there quite a long time. There was no broken glass or nothing that looked to appear to cause it: When I asked her where it came from, she said that it wasn't from that. I didn't see any other issues with that: There were no cuts or scrapes on her face, even around there, or her hands.

Prosecutor: Okay. And as a first responder and a firefighter, do you have medical training?

Firefighter: I have medical training, but I'm not medically certified.

Prosecutor: Okay. Did the face she had the type of blood on her, was that a concern for you?

Firefighter: It was because I didn't know if there was another injury that we weren't seeing.

Prosecutor: Okay. And so, based on that, what did you do, if anything?

Firefighter: So MMR did the main patient assessment, and they were treating her for that: They treated.. when they treated her, they asked me to watch her for a second while they ran to go grab some of their medical supplies. I didn't see anything on.. any cuts, scrapes, or anything where I was standing, but I didn't do a patient assessment 100 percent with.. seen most of it.

Prosecutor: Okay. And did you ever ask her, or did anybody on scene ask her where she was or what happened?

Firefighter: I did ask where she was just to see where she was in that state of mind, making sure she knew where she was at, so location: I did ask her the time and date and where, just to kind of get an idea if she was alert, oriented, and making sure she was mentally okay right there.

Prosecutor: And where did she say she was at?

Firefighter: She said she was in (REDACTED). She couldn't determine the actual road at that time.

Prosecutor: Okay. Did she say anything else about wanting help?

Firefighter: She said she would like or she wanted help, she was trying to get away, and then we – I was asking her some other questions, and while she was answering it, she asked for – she just kept repeating – I want help.

Prosecutor: Okay. And at some point, did you ever ask her her name, date of birth, those types of things?

Firefighter: I did ask her her name, date of birth, and she responded with them.

Prosecutor: And what was the name she gave you?

Firefighter: Angelee Ross, and then – I don't recall the birth date 100 percent, but it was 1980.

Prosecutor: Okay. Now, how long is this interaction with her when you've got her kind of by herself, and you're watching her while the medics are busy?

Firefighter: It was probably about seven minutes because we had a second patient, so one of the EMTs was assessing the second patient, and then the other one was grabbing the stuff from the truck.

Prosecutor: Okay. And did you continue to interact with the person that identified themselves as Angelee Ross during that time?

Firefighter: Yes, sir, I tried to communicate just to keep her awake, keep her responding so the EMT would be able to talk with her and get more information when they got back. They did bring up other stuff, events that happened that morning.

Prosecutor: Okay. What were the brought up other events that happened that morning?

Firefighter: She brought up that – all she said is I killed him at first, and then I wouldn't. Then I asked – or I asked her a couple of questions, and she responded I killed him again, and at that point, I asked "who?" thinking it was another accident scene or something that needed immediate treatment.

Prosecutor: Okay. And did she tell you who?

Firefighter: I do not recall the first name, but I remember the last name, Johnson.

Prosecutor: Okay. And at that point, what did you do with that information, if anything?

Firefighter: At that point, there was no MSP, So Michigan State Police or any law enforcement on scene, so I kept asking her, getting more information, getting another ambulance or something heading to that location just to make sure if someone was hurt that they would get treatment.

Prosecutor: Okay. And did you ever ask her to confirm or repeat either the name of the person that she claimed to have killed or the address?

Firefighter: She did give me the address; I cannot – I can't recall it offhand; I did note it in my report for that day.

Prosecutor: Okay. And do you have that report here with you?

Firefighter: I do not have it on me.

Prosecutor: Okay. Now, can you describe, you talked about her kind of going in and out, and can you give me also a description of her person: That is, what was she wearing? Give me a description of what she looked like.

Firefighter: When we initially got toned out, it was a naked female behind the driver's seat. When we got on scene, the homeowner, I believe, had put a painting gown, so like a white suit on her, to cover her up so she wasn't indecent when we got there.

Prosecutor: Okay. And you previously described the dried - what you believe to (be) dried blood: can you tell where all that appeared on her and kind of what it looked like?

Firefighter: The dried blood looked – mostly was located on her face, roughly across her eye, like above her eyebrow, and then a few other spots on her face and hands.

Prosecutor: Okay. And the person... that you interacted with, do you see that person in the courtroom here today?

Firefighter: Yes, sir.

Prosecutor: Could you please point to that person and describe what they're wearing for the record?

Firefighter: It would be the defendant in the gray jumpsuit with the orange jacket.

Prosecutor: Your Honor, please let the record reflect the witness has identified the defendant. Ms. Ross.

Judge: It shall.

Prosecutor: Thank you. Now, you said that she gave you a specific address of where this occurred?

Firefighter: Yes, sir.

Prosecutor: Okay. And if I told you that was (REDACTED), do you believe that to be accurate?

Firefighter: That sounds correct, sir.

Prosecutor: Okay. And now, did she ever reiterate to you anything else about this, or the face of who she killed and when she had done it?

Firefighter: She went and told me therefore that she.. the exact wording was she beat him until he stopped moving, stabbed him, and more, then with like kind of an odd chuckle at the end, like it's hard to describe the chuckle.

Prosecutor: Okay. Let me break down just kind of what you said. She said she beat him until he stopped moving, stabbed him, and more. And you said she had a chuckle at the end?

Firefighter: Yeah.

Prosecutor: How would you describe that?

Firefighter: It was more like a laugh, relief-type, I guess. It's hard to describe.

Prosecutor: Okay. Did that strike you as bizarre or inappropriate?

Firefighter: A little bit, considering what it was, considering what was informed to me. I didn't know 100 percent what happened, if the person was still alive, and I wanted to relay it to the other -- to the MMR truck so they could respond or have another truck respond.

Prosecutor: Okay. And did you, in fact, relay it to them?

Firefighter: I did. I asked another firefighter to keep her talking for a second: I related it to the MMR staff to let them know there was possibly something else going on.

Prosecutor: Okay. And why would you have relayed that to MMR? Would you have called dispatch yourself? Would you have relayed that to MMR? Was there a safety concern at that point?

Firefighter: I didn't have a radio with me or a cell phone, so – with me at that time, so I couldn't relay it, my personal. I did have that firefighter, when I came back, relay the plate and everything over to our Dispatch just to make sure they had the plate on file and relay --thought MMR relayed that other information.

Prosecutor: Okay. And at some point, did the Michigan State Police show up on the scene?

Firefighter: They did, roughly about seven minutes after, seven to eight minutes.

Prosecutor: Okay. So how long had you been on the scene when you provided this information related to MMR, and then MSP showed up?

Firefighter: About five minutes roughly.

Prosecutor: Okay. And do you recall who you were on – who the other first responders were that were there?

Firefighter: It would be EMT 2 – or is a paramedic, and then it would be EMT 1 as an EMT basic.

Prosecutor: Okay. And those individuals had interaction with Ms. Ross as well?

Firefighter: Yes. One of them took main contact at first with the other – with the other party...or the other patient that was injured at the time, but one of them took main contact with Ms. Ross in the back of the ambulance.

Prosecutor: So once she was placed in the ambulance, did you have any further contact with her?

Firefighter: I didn't have any further contact at that time. I gave the – once MSTP got on scene, I gave them the keys and stuff to make sure they had them so I didn't leave them in my pocket.

Prosecutor: Okay. And so she's in the ambulance, MSP is on the scene: Do you do anything else in regard to the case?

Firefighter: I looked to see if there was a driver's license to confirm the date of birth and everything on file, so – which I did not find anywhere in that car, and I looked for any other weapons that MSP would need to know.

Prosecutor: And is that – is that after MSP was already on the scene?

Firefighter: Yes.

Prosecutor: Okay. And you spoke to them?

Fire Fighter: Yes.

Prosecutor: Thank you. I don't have anything further at this time.

Judge: Ms. Defense Council?

Defense Council: Just for clarification. Sir, you stated that Ms. Ross was in and out of consciousness.

Firefighter: It was more of she was like trying to fall asleep. I wouldn't call it in and out of consciousness like a head trauma or anything like that; it was more of like she's extremely tired, and she's trying to lay her head on the steering wheel.

Defense Council: And did she look you in the eye?

Firefighter: She did.

Defense Council: Okay. And did you form any initial impressions about her mental status?

Firefighter: It seemed like someone who wanted help and needed some – needed care right there. I didn't take what she originally said as something happened right then, but when she told me exactly what happened, I wanted to relay that so we could have a second truck start heading to that location.

Defense Council: Thank you. No more questions.

Prosecutor: I don't have anything further for this witness.

Judge: Mr. Firefighter, when this individual said, "I killed him," was that in response to a question you had asked?

Firefighter: No, sir, it was more of a... more of a remark than anything else.

Judge: Thank you, Mr. Firefighter. You are free to go about your day.

Chapter 10: EMT 1

Prosecutor: Your Honor, I would call EMT 1 to the stand.

Clerk: EMT 1, would you please raise your right hand? Do you solemnly swear or affirm that the testimony you give in this case will be the truth, the whole truth, and nothing but the truth, so help you God?

EMT 1: Yes.

Judge: You can have a seat right next (to) me, Ms. EMT 1. Good morning.

Prosecutor: Good morning, EMT 1. Could you please state and spell your name for the record?

EMT 1: (REDACTED).

Prosecutor: And Ms. EMT 1, what is your occupation, for whom do you work?

EMT 1: I'm an EMT, and I work for Mobile Medical Response.

Prosecutor: Okay. And were you working for Mobile Medical Response in the capacity of an EMT on March 17th, 2021, that morning?

EMT 1: Yes.

Prosecutor: Okay. Is there something that happened on that date at approximately 7:50 in the morning?

EMT 1: Yes. We got called to a vehicle accident in (REDACTED).

Prosecutor: And would that have been at (REDACTED)?

EMT 1: I believe so, yes.

Prosecutor: Okay. And what did you find when you arrived?

EMT 1: When we pulled in, there were multiple vehicles in the driveway. We had seen an SUV and a midsize car, and the SUV had rear-ended the car in the driveway.

Prosecutor: And when you got on scene, what did you do?

EMT 1: My partner went to the vehicles, and there were other victims standing to the side, so I approached the victim standing to the side that had been struck in the midsize car.

Prosecutor: And so you tended to those individuals?

EMT 1: Correct.

Prosecutor: And your partner was who?

EMT 1: EMT 2.

Prosecutor: And EMT 2, what did he do at that point?

EMT 1: He went up to the SUV, to the driver's side, and tended to that patient in the SUV.

Prosecutor: And how long were you with the individuals that you were tending to?

EMT 1: Most of the time, we were on scene. My partner EMT 2 pulled me aside after I made sure my patients were cared for, and he informed me of what the patient and his patient had informed him, and from there, we loaded the patient and left the scene.

Prosecutor: And when you say we loaded the patient, this is the patient that was in the SUV?

EMT 1: Correct.

Prosecutor: And who was that person?

EMT 1: I believe Ms. Ross.

Prosecutor: And do you see Ms. Ross in the courtroom here today? Would you please point to her and describe what she's wearing for the record?

EMT 1: Yes. She's in the orange jacket.

Prosecutor: Thank you. Your Honor, please let the record reflect that the witness has identified the defendant.

MY FATHER'S STORY

Judge: It shall.

Prosecutor: Now, EMT 1, once you got her loaded into the ambulance, what did you do?

EMT 1: I put our blood pressure cuff on her and started taking vital signs.

Prosecutor: Okay. Did you have concerns about her medical condition at that point?

EMT 1: She had a fair amount of blood on her that we - I had not taken care of her at the time, so I did not know where it came from. I was not privy to the beginning of that assessment. So her vital signs were stable, but I had no - didn't have any information about her medical condition.

Prosecutor: What about her behavior? Can you tell me about that?

EMT 1: Yes. She was mumbling incoherently at times, just words that didn't necessarily make sense.

Prosecutor: Okay. Was she conscious? Was she alert?

EMT 1: She was conscious and alert, and she had - we asked her with every patient we always ask do you know your name, your birth date, where you're at, what day it is, stuff like that, and she answered all those appropriately.

Prosecutor: Okay. And so you got the blood pressure cuff on her, took her blood pressure, what did you do then?

EMT 1: Then I went and drove us to the hospital: My partner attended in the back of the ambulance.

Prosecutor: Okay. And while you were on your way to the hospital, do you know, did she make any statements to you or to anybody that was in the ambulance that you heard?

EMT 1: Yes. When I was in the back, she also made comments, she admitted to us that she had killed a male subject at a different residence.

Prosecutor: Okay. And did she say where that was?

EMT 1: She did, and I have a statement that I wrote for the court on that day, and I'm not familiar with the address, but it's in my statement: I believe it was (REDACTED).

Prosecutor: Now, did she indicate to you who she had killed?

EMT 1: I believe she said the name was William Johnson.

Prosecutor: And so once you had that information, what did you do? Did you do anything with that information, or had that already been dealt with?

EMT 1: The other patient, you mean?

Prosecutor: No, the information that she had killed William Johnson on (REDACTED).

EMT 1: My partner, before we loaded her into the truck, had told me that she had admitted that to him in the SUV, so I was already aware, and then she told it to me, and we had officers with us at the time.

Prosecutor: So, were there officers in the back of the ambulance as well?

EMT 1: Yes, they were with us the entire call.

Prosecutor: And those would have been Michigan State Police Troopers?

EMT 1: Correct.

Prosecutor: Okay. Now, you said that she was mumbling somewhat unintelligibly on the way: Did you make out anything that she had said?

EMT 1: She had made comments about wanting us to take her to Florida. I don't know the relevance of that, but and then when we had gotten to the ER, she had thanked us for doing God's work, and she had mumbled other comments about stuff, God's work, but nothing that I can recall at this time.

Prosecutor: Do you recall – I mean, your interactions with her, were they - were they interactions of a normal patient or did she appear off to you?

EMT 1: She appeared off.

Prosecutor: Why do you say that?

EMT 1: Because she appeared to be trying to think of the word, sorry. She appeared to be almost frantic a little bit: She was repeating herself over and over: Like I said, she had told us a few times that she killed him, "I killed him, can you take me to Florida?" and she was just kind of bouncing around with her words.

Prosecutor: And what about – what about her state of dress, what was she wearing?

EMT 1: So when we got to her, when my partner had got to her, she was in a white Tyvek suit. The family that I had spoken to on the scene stated that when they struck her - when she struck their vehicle she was naked, and they had a Tyvek suit available, so they provided her with that.

Prosecutor: Okay. And during the course of your treatment, I know you had indicated that she had dried blood on her, can you tell me, if you recall, the places that you recall seeing dried blood on her?

EMT 1: I cannot.

Prosecutor: Did she have dried blood on her face, do you know?

EMT 1: She did have dried blood on her face, and it appeared to be on her hands as well, but I don't know anywhere else besides that.

Prosecutor: Okay. And you probably... you would not have had contact with any other areas of her?

EMT 1: No. And I don't believe my partner did either. She was in that... like I said, she was in a Tyvek suit when we got to her.

Prosecutor: And what happened when you got to the hospital?

EMT 1: We brought her into the emergency department, and my partner gave a report – my partner gave a report to (REDACTED), who then took over her care.

Prosecutor: Okay. And would that have been the extent of your contact with her as well as anything to do with this motor vehicle accident?

EMT 1: Correct.

Prosecutor: Thank you. I don't have anything further.

Defense Council: No questions, Your Honor.

Judge: Thank you, Ms. EMT 1. You're free to go about your day.

Chapter 11: EMT 2

Prosecutor: Your Honor, I would like to call EMT 2 to the stand.

Clerk: EMT 2, would you please raise your right hand? Do you solemnly swear or affirm that the testimony you give in this cause will be the truth, the whole truth, and nothing but the truth, so help you God?

EMT 2: Yes.

Judge: You can have a seat right next to me, EMT 2. Good morning.

Prosecutor: Good Morning, EMT 2. Could you state and spell your name for the record?

EMT 2: (REDACTED)

Prosecutor: Sir, what is your occupation, for whom do you work?

EMT 2: I work for the city of Manistee Fire Department as a firefighter/paramedic currently.

Prosecutor: And as of March 17th of 2021, what were you employed as?

EMT 2: I was employed as a full-time paramedic with MMR.

MY FATHER'S STORY

Prosecutor: Now, I want to ask you about the date of March 17th, 2021. Is there something that happened on that date about 7:30 in the morning or shortly thereafter?

EMT 2: We were dispatched to what was originally reported as a PL accident.

Prosecutor: And where was that?

EMT 2: I believe that was in (REDACTED).

Prosecutor: Now, what happened when you arrived on the scene? What did you see?

EMT 2: There were two vehicles in a driveway near each other, one with its front bumper into the rear bumper of the other vehicle. The occupants of the first vehicle, from what I witnessed, were all out of the vehicle and standing. I do believe they came out of their garage or their home when we arrived on the scene.

Prosecutor: And you made contact with them, correct?

EMT 2: Yes.

Prosecutor: And what happened after that?

EMT 2: Usually, in a vehicle crash where there are multiple patients, we do an initial triage. People that are typically walking and ambulating, and talking, generally get a lower priority, and as such, I assigned my partner to further triage those patients, and I approached the second vehicle to look at the occupant of that vehicle.

Prosecutor: And the second vehicle was what type of vehicle and what color, if you recall?

EMT 2: I can't recall at the present time.

Prosecutor: Do you know what type of vehicle it was? Was it a SUV?

EMT 2: I believe so, yes.

Prosecutor: And what can you tell me about the occupant of that vehicle?

EMT 2: On our arrival, the patient was wearing a Tyvek suit, much like a painter would wear or, you know, someone that deals with chemicals. She was slumped to the right side and appeared initially lethargic, somewhat unresponsive, but when we made access to the vehicle, she roused fairly easily.

Prosecutor: And can you describe that, how was she roused?

EMT 2: Typically, we start with verbal, we call the patient, and if that doesn't work, then we might tap them on the shoulder, give them a little shake; if that doesn't work, then we do what we call painful stimuli which is usually like a sternal rub. And with just a loud voice and a slight touch, she kind of sat up.

Prosecutor: Okay. And what was your interaction with her at that point?

MY FATHER'S STORY

EMT 2: At that point, she, to me, appeared to be altered such that she was the most priority patient of the patients at that scene, and therefore, as the highest level of licensure, she would be the patient I would be administering first care to.

Prosecutor: And when you say altered, what do you mean by altered? What is that? What does that mean? Is that a medical term?

EMT 2: Yeah, that's generally someone who is either confused or lethargic, they can be alert but not making sense, and the things they're saying or the things they're doing are just generally altered from what we would call a normal mentation.

Prosecutor: Okay. And those are things that you observed about her?

EMT 2: Yes.

Prosecutor: Was she saying anything that wasn't making sense to you?

EMT 2: At that point, no. Later in our interactions, she did say some things that did not make sense to me, that seemed a little bit altered further at that point.

Prosecutor: Well, take me through at that point: So she's roused, what happens then?

EMT 2: We usually start - in EMS, we kind of start with the simplest problem and work further down. She was nude upon arrival to the scene. She was dressed in a Tyvek suit, but that was, I guess, provided to her; so based on that, the location of the crash and just her general appearance to me suggested some type of substance might be or she could be hypoglycemic or hyperglycemic, we can't test in the field for the presence of any type of drug or alcohol, so usually our first go-to is to do a blood sugar check. We did the blood sugar check that came back - I can't remember the exact value, but it came back within a range that did not have me too terribly concerned, but as we were performing that and we did a little finger poke, I did notice there was blood on and under her fingers and that blood was not really consistent with the type of crash that had occurred: You would expect to see that If there were broken windows or like a shattered windshield, something like that.

Prosecutor: Okay. And you said that blood wasn't consistent: consistent how? Is it the way that it's displayed on the body, or is it?

EMT 2: Yeah. So it was more like aerosolized blood, almost like a splatter or a spatter that would not be really consistent with a low-speed mechanism of injury or MOI; that would be more consistent with something at a higher speed that could project that blood outward.

MY FATHER'S STORY

Prosecutor: And so at that point, were you concerned about that, that there may be other injuries from something else on the patient?

EMT 2: Yeah, I was concerned that there - she may be, again, with an altered mental status. I was concerned that maybe she wasn't aware that something had occurred to her, so or that maybe something had happened to her prior to her arriving at that location, and I began to ask her if she was hurting anywhere, if she was having our general kind of assessment questions and that kind of goes at the same time we're performing other things, so I can't give you the exact order of everything. And she, from what I can recall, she did not say that she was injured.

Prosecutor: Okay. And so when you do the glucose test, I guess, to make sure she's not in what, diabetic shock?

EMT 2: Yeah.

Prosecutor: Is she still in the vehicle at this point?

EMT 2: Yes, she's still there. She remained in the vehicle for some time, I can't give you an exact time frame without looking at the times of the call specifically, but she was in there for what I would estimate probably 10 to 15 minutes total.

Prosecutor: And were you with her that whole time?

EMT 2: I did step away to make a phone call.

Prosecutor: Now, when you're interacting with her, tell me about whether or not did you have any discussions with her?

EMT 2: We did. I had asked her where that blood came from and if she was injured because I said, you know, that's quite a bit of blood, it's not likely that that occurred from this crash. Do you happen to know where it came from? At this point, she did tell me that she had murdered someone.

Prosecutor: And did she tell you who she had murdered?

EMT 2: Yes, she did.

Prosecutor: And who did she say that she had murdered?

EMT 2: I can't recall off the top of my head; I know that would be in my statement.

Prosecutor: Okay. And if you looked at that, would that refresh your recollection?

EMT 2: Yes, absolutely.

Prosecutor: May I approach the witness? EMT 2, if you could please review that statement specifically as it relates to the question and let me know when you're done if it has refreshed your recollection?

EMT 2: I'm scanning through this for you. I do not see that in there: however, I believe, in hindsight, I did omit

MY FATHER'S STORY

that for the simple fact that I did not want to give the wrong name or spelling under the assumption that this, in fact, would be going to court, so apologies.

Prosecutor: Understood. And do you know if she indicated to you ever where that this murder occurred?

EMT 2: Yes, she did give me a name and an address. I then proceeded to do a few more assessment things as sometimes it's been my experience that patients can say things, whether intentionally or not, to just kind of cause chaos on the scene, especially if someone has an altered mental status or is confused. At this point, after performing a few more assessment items, I asked her again to repeat it to me just to see if everything lined back up. It did, in fact, and that was at the point that I stepped away and had one of the first responders maintain contact with the patient while I called Manistee Central Dispatch.

Prosecutor: And that first responder has been Firefighter?

EMT 2: It was.

Prosecutor: Okay. And so you called Central Dispatch, and you advised Central Dispatch basically what?

EMT 2: I repeated what the patient had said to me with name, address, and that central -- whether or not this was, in fact, a true statement or not, I advised central that it would probably be best to send either a trooper or an officer or a deputy out that way to investigate that scene.

Prosecutor: Okay. And did they, in fact, send troopers to your scene as well?

EMT 2: I received that knowledge secondhand. They said they would send someone out there, but I was not in further contact with Manistee Central Dispatch after that point.

Prosecutor: Did MSP troopers show up on the scene?

EMT 2: They did. Shortly after I made that phone call, two troopers arrived, and as I was hanging up the phone with Manistee Central Dispatch, they approached the ambulance. I kind of gave them a quick rundown of what I'd assessed so far and what was said to me just so that they would be aware as well.

Prosecutor: And while you were in the ambulance, did you treat the patient or was that your partner?

EMT 2: I provide – when the patient is under my care, until I pass that off, the patient remains under my care. My partner was in there at some points throughout the interaction with the patient, as were troopers, but primary care was initiated and maintained by myself.

Prosecutor: And at some point, you identified the patient? And the patient was who?

EMT 2: The defendant sitting here.

Prosecutor: Ms. Ross?

EMT 2: Yes.

Prosecutor: Now, in your interactions with Ms. Ross. While you were in the ambulance, did she say anything else to you?

EMT 2: She did make several statements, and I didn't quote all of them simply because I didn't want to get them out of context, but the one is, as in my statement here, is that she was performing God's work and doing the right thing.

Prosecutor: Okay. And did she ever discuss at any point while she was in the ambulance to your recollection, did she ever discuss the murder again?

EMT 2: She did not, no. I tried to... it has also been my experience that keeping patients calm, she was very cooperative with us, at no point was I fearful for my safety, my partner's safety, or anyone else's, but it has been my experience that patients can – especially those that are altered mental status and confused, can become irritable quickly. So as she made certain statements, I just kind of let them slide, made casual conversation with her for the duration of our time. I didn't inquire any further into the statement about a murder. I did not feel that would be beneficial to me or her in a medical capacity.

Prosecutor: Okay. So was there a concern that you didn't want to set anything off?

EMT 2: Correct, yes. I did not want to get the patient riled up or potentially endanger myself or anyone else: I was not directly fearful of that, but it's also been my experience that with, say, someone under the influence of an illicit substance can become irritable quite quickly.

Prosecutor: And did you notice any mood swings with Ms. Ross?

EMT 2: I did not. She did become a little bit emotional throughout our encounter. At some points, she was tearful, but I did not notice any violent mood swings towards me or my partners or anyone else involved in her care.

Prosecutor: Tell me about her overall behavior. Is there anything that struck you about just her overall behavior and demeanor?

EMT 2: I'm not really sure how much I'm able to project my medical impression, but.. okay. So as a – from a medical standpoint, based on what she had told me and what I had experienced with her, she seemed to be in a state of shock, that would be my... my primary impression, as we call it, is the thing we would be most looking at medically to treat for. She was making statements that didn't seem to make sense. She did not openly seem remorseful, but she didn't seem vengeful, it just seemed like a very flat effect.

Prosecutor: Is that when she was discussing the murder?

EMT 2: She was discussing... Oh, initially, yes, when she mentioned it to me.

Prosecutor: She was a flat affect when she mentioned that?

EMT 2: Yes.

Prosecutor: Matter of fact?

EMT 2: Yes.

Prosecutor: Is there anything else about her behavior that would have struck you as odd?

EMT 2: In our interactions, she.. she seemed, like I said, very flat in her responses to me and the way she was acting, but again, nothing that stood out to me to be incredibly violent or what you might consider like a manic depressive-type where she was incredibly sad and then back to being agitated or anything like that, just remained very curt, yes, very, very simple answers.

Prosecutor: And you had indicated that she did have blood that you had seen on her, dried blood: can you tell me all the places that you saw that on her?

EMT 2: I do believe I saw some on her face with the troopers. We did kind of take the Tyvek suit off, we did leave the doors slightly ajar to open, just given the nature of the incident and my concern that perhaps something later down the line could be said that was going on in the ambulance. We did cover the patient as best as possible with blankets, but we did notice some blood further up her arms. I believe there was some. Yeah, I do believe we found some bruising bilaterally or scratches on the upper arms, but most of the blood was located bilaterally on the hands and arms, the face, and the neck area.

Prosecutor: Okay. Thank you. I don't have anything further at this time.

Defense Council: Just one question, EMT 2. In your report, you indicated that she stated she did not know her location or how she arrived there. Is that correct?

EMT 2: Yes.

Defense Council: Okay. And did she ever realize where she was or how she had gotten there in your presence?

EMT 2: I don't believe that we ever discussed that much further, but she never openly said to me that she knew where she was at. Usually, we follow that up a couple of times to see if we're making progress with the patient's mentatlon, and I don't recall her ever giving me a solid answer on that.

Defense Council: Okay, Thank you very much. Nothing further.

Judge: EMT 2, you're excused from subpoena. Please do not discuss your testimony with anyone.

Chapter 12: Trooper 1

Prosecutor: Your Honor, I would call Trooper 1 to the stand.

Clerk: Would you please raise your right hand? Do you solemnly swear or affirm that the testimony you give in this cause will be the truth, the whole truth, and nothing but the truth, so help you God?

Trooper 1: Yes, ma'am, I do.

Judge: Good Morning.

Prosecutor: Good Morning, Trooper 1. Could you please state and spell your name for the record?

Trooper 1: Yes, (REDACTED).

Prosecutor: And Trooper 1, what is your occupation? For whom do you work?

Trooper 1: I am a trooper for the Michigan State Police out of the Cadillac post.

Prosecutor: Okay. And were you working on the morning of March 17th, 2021?

Trooper 1: Yes, sir, I was.

Prosecutor: Okay. And is there something that happened on that date on that morning?

Trooper 1: Yes, sir. On the morning of March 17th of, 2021, I was dispatched to, basically, a fender bender at a residence. It was a property, a private property. Upon arrival, you don't mind if I can look at my report?

Prosecutor: Do you need to refresh your recollection? Did you write a report on this matter?

Trooper 1: Yes, sir, I did. Upon arrival, I saw two vehicles: I saw a green Chevrolet Tahoe, a female was in the front seat, and she did have a gown on. I did not make contact with her at this point. I kind of just observed her: EMS was working with her, and she was kind of in and out of consciousness.

Prosecutor: Did you know what you were dealing with at this point in time, or was it just a fender bender in your mind?

Trooper 1: In my mind, it was just, yeah, a private property crash.

Prosecutor: Please continue.

Trooper 1: So after that, I had made contact with an EMS worker, I believe his name was EMT 2. I made contact with him: He had advised that she was making statements....Angelee Ross, she was making statements having killed a man. She even gave a name, she gave an address. At that point, I waited until she was loaded in the ambulance, and that's when I made contact with her.

Prosecutor: And what can you tell me about that contact with her?

Trooper 1: So I made contact with her. I can identify her, she's right there, Angelee Ross, and when I made contact with her, I identified myself as Trooper 1, and I just asked her what happened, and she goes like, "I killed him" and I asked, "You killed who?", she stated "William Johnson." At that point, I had asked, "With what?" she stated anything that she could get her hands on, and then I asked for the address, which she was able to provide me.

Prosecutor: And what was that address that she provided to you?

Trooper 1: Yeah. So that address that was given to me was (REDACTED).

Prosecutor: And what did you do with that information?

Trooper 1: I notified the other trooper that was with me at the time. I know dispatch was well aware from the EMS worker that had contacted them, and we had sent additional units out to that address.

Prosecutor: Okay. And so once she had indicated that she had killed William Johnson and given you the address that it happened, did she say anything else?

Trooper 1: No, not that I can recall.

Prosecutor: What was her demeanor like when she was telling you about this?

Trooper 1: So when she was speaking to me, she kind of seemed in and out of it at times, but when I was asking her direct questions, she would look directly at me, she would answer them, there was no hesitation. Any questions that I asked her, she provided me with the answers.

Prosecutor: Okay. What was her effect? Did she have a flat affect, was she emotional? How did she respond?

Trooper 1: There was a lack of emotion, there was really none. It was just having a conversation and her giving me direct answers.

Prosecutor: Okay. Matter-of-fact, direct answers?

Trooper 1: Yes.

Prosecutor: How long did you interact with her last when you were having this contact with her?

Trooper 1: I would say about several minutes. It all happened pretty fast, actually.

Prosecutor: Other than what she was telling you, was there anything about her behavior that struck you as odd or off?

MY FATHER'S STORY

Trooper 1: Other than her being in and out of consciousness, no. It was just one general tone answering my questions, there was nothing particularly odd other than that, but the fact that she had just rear-ended somebody, you know, I didn't know if it was because of that; so, you know, she seemed in and out of consciousness, but when it came to answering my questions she was very direct. There was nothing more unusual than that.

Prosecutor: What about her appearance? Can you describe her appearance for the court?

Trooper 1: Yes. So when I first noticed her, I notice her in the vehicle. She did have a white gown on, which I believe the residents - the owner provided her. When she was in the ambulance, I noticed she did have blood on her. I didn't notice anything else, maybe.. maybe some bruising to the arms.

Prosecutor: Okay. And at some point while you're on the scene, did you ask to provide information that you have based upon your experience from the crash? Find out that what she had told you actually there was evidence to back that up.

Trooper 1: Yes. While on the scene, we had been advised by dispatch that it appeared at that address that something had occurred, so at that point, we kind of knew that what she was telling us was true, and then after that, I ended up going to that residence where the crime occurred.

Prosecutor: Okay. You went to the (REDACTED) residence?

Trooper 1: Yes, sir, that is correct.

Prosecutor: And what did you do when you got to the (REDACTED) address?

Trooper 1: When I went to the (REDACTED) address, I did not go inside: I actually assisted Trooper 2 with the search warrant, and we waited for the lab to arrive.

Prosecutor: So you assist Trooper 2. Is that just to provide him information that you have based upon your experience from the crash?

Trooper 1: Yes, from the initial scene, yes.

Prosecutor: And did you previously make a statement about ID, but do you see the person in the courtroom today that had indicated to you that they had killed Mr. William Johnson at the (REDACTED) address?

Trooper 1: Yes, sir, right in front of me in the orange jacket.

Prosecutor: Your Honor, please let the record reflect the witness has identified the defendant.

Judge: It shall.

MY FATHER'S STORY

Prosecutor: Trooper 1, I've handed you what has previously been marked People's Proposed Exhibit Number 1. Can you tell me if you recognize that?

Trooper 1: I recognize both vehicles.

Prosecutor: And what is that? Is that a photograph?

Trooper 1: Yes, sir, it is. So it's a photograph of what I was actually dispatched to, which was the PDA.

Prosecutor: And is that a fair and accurate representation of how those vehicles looked on that day and how they were when you arrived?

Trooper 1: Yes, sir.

Prosecutor: And can you describe what is in the photo?

Trooper 1: From the photo, I see .. well, I see three vehicles, the gray pick-up truck that was not involved in the crash, the Chevy Tahoe, and then I can't make out the description of the passenger vehicle, but those are the two vehicles that were involved in the PDA.

Prosecutor: And Ms. Ross was the driver of the Tahoe?

Trooper 1: Yes, that's correct.

Prosecutor: Your Honor, I'd move to admit People's Proposed Exhibit Number 1 into evidence at this time.

Judge: People's Exhibit 1 is received.

Prosecutor: Trooper 1, did you have a chance to really note Ms. Ross' physical appearance, that is, the appearance of any blood, of any potential injuries and those types of things?

Trooper 1: Yes. I know I noted them in my report if I could take a look at that.

Prosecutor: Okay. So did you, in fact, note things regarding her physical appearance?

Trooper 1: Yes. So in my report, I noted injuries and observations. I noticed dried blood on the head and face: In addition, I observed blood dried on the left palm as well and underneath both fingernails, and then also blue and purple color above the left wrist. I observed bruises and a puncture in the center of the left forearm and then dried blood above the right elbow and right ankle.

Prosecutor: Now, at some point, Ms. Ross was taken via ambulance to Munson Manistee Medical Center, is that correct? And did you accompany her in the ambulance at that time?

Trooper 1: Yes, sir, that's correct. No, sir.

Prosecutor: Was there a trooper that would have ridden in the ambulance, or was there a trooper that would have met them at the hospital?

Trooper 1: A trooper, I believe, did meet her at the hospital.

Prosecutor: Okay. But nobody, to your knowledge, had ridden in the ambulance.

Trooper 1: No, not to my knowledge.

Prosecutor: And would that – would that be a normal thing to do?

Trooper 1: Depends on the circumstances. Given in that one, we decided to go to the actual address (REDACTED), as opposed to going to the hospital.

Prosecutor: Thank you. I don't have anything further.

Defense Council: Thank you. Trooper 1, you also interviewed other individuals at the scene, didn't you?

Trooper 1: Yes, ma'am, that's true.

Defense Council: And in particular, you interviewed Mrs. Grandpa?

Trooper 1: I believe so, yes.

Defense Council: And she was a homeowner where the car was located?

Trooper 1: That's correct, yes, ma'am.

Defense Council: And do you recall what she told you about the female that she encountered in the car that struck their family car?

Trooper 1: I do not remember a whole lot from that interview.

Defense Council: May I approach, Your Honor. (Hands Trooper 1 her report.)

Trooper 1: It looks as if another Trooper might have been the lead in speaking with her.

Defense Council: So you don't recall that you interviewed Mrs. Grandpa?

Trooper 1: No. I may have made contact with her, but in terms of an actual interview, it looks as If this is another Trooper.

Defense Council: Okay. Thank you. Trooper 1, did you interview Brad (REDACTED)?

Trooper 1: Would that be the Auto Value worker?

Defense Council: Yes.

Trooper 1: Yes, I did speak to him.

Defense Council: So you interviewed Mr. Brad on March 17th, 2021?

MY FATHER'S STORY

Trooper 1: Yes, ma'am, that's correct.

Defense Council: And can you tell us how Mr. Brad was related in any way to Mr. William Johnson?

Trooper 1: So he was the manager at the Auto Store in Manistee or is, I guess I should say.

Defense Council: Yes. And he informed you, did he not, that Mr. Johnson had been an employee at that establishment since approximately 2018?

Trooper 1: Yes, ma'am, that's correct.

Defense Council: That he'd been a model employee?

Trooper 1: Yes, that's correct.

Defense Council: And was always routinely very early to work, correct?

Trooper 1: Yes, ma'am.

Defense Council: And Mr. Brad told you that he was aware that Ms. Ross had come over from Cadillac to Mr. Johnson's home on Sunday night, March 14th, correct?

Trooper 1: Yes, ma'am.

Defense Council: And Mr. Johnson told Mr. Brad that, on Sunday, Ms. Ross had removed smoke alarms from his home?

Trooper 1: That's correct, yes, ma'am.

Defense Council: And that she'd unplugged the microwave?

Trooper 1: That's correct.

Defense Council: And anything else that was plugged in?

Trooper 1: Yes, ma'am.

Defense Council: And that, he said, was because Ms. Ross thought people were listening?

Trooper 1: That's correct.

Defense Council: And that a space shuttle was coming?

Trooper 1: Yes, ma'am.

Defense Council: And the purge was happening?

Trooper 1: That's correct.

Defense Council: And then the following morning at about 5:20 .. or 5:52, Mr. Johnson left a voice message for his boss Mr. Brad, correct?

Trooper 1: That's correct.

Defense Council: And he was advising that he was going to stay home that day due to personal issues involving Ms. Ross, correct?

Trooper 1: Yes, ma'am, that's correct.

Defense Council: And Mr. Brad found this very odd, correct? Because Mr. Johnson never had called in sick prior to that?

Trooper 1: Yes, ma'am.

Defense Council: All right. He also told you that Mr. Johnson commented that there was no power at his residence. Is that correct?

Trooper 1: Yes, ma'am, that is.

Defense Council: But did not know why. Is that correct?

Trooper 1: Yes.

Defense Council: Okay. Nothing further.

Prosecutor: I have no further questions for this witness.

Judge: The court would just note that the questions that Ms. Defense Council just asked of Trooper 1, I'm already familiar with some of that evidence as a result of the stipulated exhibit that the parties asked the court to review last week, and so I am familiar with that testimony. You are excused from your subpoena. Just please do not talk about your testimony with any other potential witnesses.

Chapter 13: Trooper 2

Prosecutor: Your Honor, I would call Trooper 2 to the stand.

Clerk: Would you please raise your right hand? Do you solemnly swear or affirm that the testimony you give in this case will be the truth, the whole truth, and nothing but the truth, so help you God?

Trooper 2: I do.

Prosecutor: Good Morning. Sir, could you please state and spell your name for the record?

Trooper 2: My name is (REDACTED).

Prosecutor: And sir, what is your occupation, for whom do you work?

Trooper 2: I'm a trooper with the Michigan State Police, Cadillac post.

Prosecutor: And as a trooper with the Michigan State Police, what kind of training do you have?

Trooper 2: Been through the Michigan State Police Trooper Recruit School, Advanced Trooper School, and Basic Investigators School.

Prosecutor: And do you have any EMS or EMT training?

Trooper 2: Yes, I was a licensed paramedic in the state of Michigan for nine years.

Prosecutor: Okay. I want to ask you about March 17th, 2021, the morning of that date: Did anything happen on that date and that morning?

Trooper 2: Yes.

Prosecutor: Please tell me what happened.

Trooper 2: I was working in the county of Manistee. I responded with Trooper 3 to check the well-being of (REDACTED) here in Manistee County.

Prosecutor: And do you recall that exact address on (REDACTED)?

Trooper 2: I believe it was (REDACTED) if I recall correctly.

Prosecutor: And what did you find when you arrived at that well-being check?

Trooper 2: Trooper 3 was just ahead of me, we roughly arrived at the same time and found the garage door to the residence open: It looked fairly well kept, except for there was a large blanket in the middle of the garage, which seemed to be out of place. I went around the back side of the house while Trooper 3 attempted to contact the door. When I went around the back, I noticed a hole in a second-floor window. There were a lot of glass windows, which looked like possibly cathedral ceilings.

Prosecutor: You indicated that there was a hole in the glass: What type of hole? What did it appear to you to be?

Trooper 2: It was a small round hole. I believe - I wasn't 100 percent sure because we were still investigating, but it looked like it could be consistent with a gunshot.

Prosecutor: And you're on the ground at this point: How high up is that hole, and how high up is that window?

Trooper 2: Probably at least I'd say 12 feet.

Prosecutor: Okay. And so once you saw that, what did you do?

Trooper 2: At that time, Trooper 3 called out to me that he had blood on the inside entry door to the garage between the garage and the house.

Prosecutor: Okay. And was the garage door open when you arrived?

Trooper 2: Yes, the main garage door was open, yes.

Prosecutor: Okay. And so, did you join Trooper 3 at that point?

Trooper 2: Yes.

Prosecutor: Okay. Tell what happened then.

Trooper 2: So we made entry into the garage, into the house, immediately saw that there was a lot of blood on the walls as we were making entry just as soon as we came through the door.

Prosecutor: And can you describe the layout of the interior of the residence: You come in the door, and now this door is through the garage that enters the home?

Trooper 2: Yes.

Prosecutor: Okay. So kind of take me through what the layout of the main floor of the residence is.

Trooper 2: So, when we made entry through the garage, there were immediately two bedrooms on our right: When we got to the second bedroom, the hallway made an L-shape to go into the rest of the house: we were at kind of at the corner of the L, looked to the right, and we could see a dead dog just lying there in the second bedroom.

Prosecutor: And you indicated that, in that entryway, there was blood all over the place?

Trooper 2: Yes.

Prosecutor: Did you go into that second bedroom at that point?

Trooper 2: Yes.

Prosecutor: And did you see anything else other than the deceased dog?

Trooper 2: Not that I recall at this time.

Prosecutor: Where was the dog located in the bedroom?

Trooper 2: It was just inside the doors lying on the ground between the bed and wall.

Prosecutor: And do you recall what type of dog that was?

Trooper 2: It was a large dog, I couldn't see for sure, but maybe like a pit bull or something similar to that.

Prosecutor: But it was a large dog?

Trooper 2: Yes.

Prosecutor: So you see the second bedroom on the right, there's a dog, what do you do then?

Trooper 2: So at this point, Trooper 3 and I are proceeding through the house, he was ahead of me: As we're coming through the hallway to get to the kitchen area, I noticed there was a - there was a lot of things in disarray as if there had been a struggle; however, it stood out to me that there was the victim's wallet and a driver's license which was - seemed to be, just laying right in the middle of the hallway almost like somebody had placed it there was my impression. So that stood out to me. When we got to the kitchen, Trooper 3 was looking left or kind of handling stuff on the left side of the room. I took the right, and I could see the whole house was in disarray: I also noted a handgun lying on the kitchen counter.

Prosecutor: Okay. And when you say the whole house was in disarray, just kind of paint a picture for me as to what you're seeing at that point: I mean, are we talking about furniture flipped over and that stuff? Do you notice any blood anywhere?

Trooper 2: I...Trooper 3 found - I just remember the blood in the hallways as we're coming in. There was a lot in the initial entry, and then when Trooper 3 found the victim at the bottom of the stairs, which is also kind of in the same living room/kitchen area, it's a large open area, pretty much one room, there was a significant amount of blood around the victim.

Prosecutor: Okay. And you had indicated that Trooper 3 had found the victim: Did he notify you as soon as that had happened?

Trooper 2: Yes.

Prosecutor: Okay. And did you proceed to that area of the home?

Trooper 2: Yes.

Prosecutor: And what did you do, if anything? Was there a concern at this point that emergency medical assistance would be needed?

Trooper 2: Well, I went to feel his neck and checked for a carotid pulse: At that point, I realized that his jaw was stiff, his neck was stiff, and I also noted large lacerations to his neck, and based on my training and experience the stiffness comes from rigor mortis, and so at that point, there are no life-saving measures that can be helpful at that point.

Prosecutor: And it was your belief and understanding that he was deceased at that point?

Trooper 2: That's correct.

Prosecutor: And there was no question in your mind as to that?

Trooper 2: No.

Prosecutor: Okay. So, once you established that, what did you do then?

Trooper 2: We continued our search. We still had the second floor. There was – he was at the bottom of the stairs, so we continued up the stairs: At this point, I was in front of Trooper 3. We got to the top of the stairs and found a second – it was a large, open room with a few small rooms along the side. We found a second deceased dog.

Prosecutor: And do you know - what can you tell me about the appearance of that dog?

Trooper 2: Several stab wounds to the torso, or what appeared to be stab wounds to the torso of the dog.

Prosecutor: And did you notice anything else in that room?

Trooper 2: I saw a knife.

Prosecutor: Can you describe the knife and where it was in the room?

Trooper 2: I remember - I believe, if I remember correctly, it was on the bed, just kind of laying out. It's about all I remember.

Prosecutor: And do you know, was it a fixed-blade knife, was it a kitchen knife?

Trooper 2: Yeah, I believe it was a large, fixed-blade kitchen or butcher knife.

Prosecutor: Okay. And you said the upstairs was one - one large room with a couple smaller - what were a couple of smaller rooms that were off of the large room?

Trooper 2: If I remember correctly, maybe a closet and maybe a bathroom.

Prosecutor: Okay. So it was basically a bedroom upstairs with an on-suite bathroom and closet, if you will?

Trooper 2: That's how I recall it, yes.

Prosecutor: And where was the victim in relation to the stairs?

Trooper 2: So he was at the bottom of the stairs.

Prosecutor: And you had already indicated, Trooper 2, that there were... that there was a handgun that you had found, I believe, on the kitchen counter?

Trooper 2: Yes.

Prosecutor: Did you locate any other weapons in the residence at that time, or did you view any other weapons?

Trooper 2: Yes.

Prosecutor: What did you find?

Trooper 2: There was a second handgun lying next to the victim.

Prosecutor: And what color was that handgun?

Trooper 2: It was black.

Prosecutor: Okay. Well, let me get to this: What was the purpose at this point of you and Trooper 3 going through the residence? Was this? Was this a protective sweep? Was there a concern that there might be somebody else still in there, or were you collecting evidence at this time?

MY FATHER'S STORY

Trooper 2: We were concerned, obviously there was - we'd gone through the first time for exigent circumstances, we see the blood on the door, concerned about the victim's well-being. The second sweep is, once we realize we have a crime scene, we want to make sure we didn't miss anybody or a second victim, so we go through a second time to make sure we were thorough, that we didn't miss any other closets or small spaces like under the bed just to make sure that we had covered all of our bases, then we backed out.

Prosecutor: You backed out. Is it the policy at this that, really, you don't touch anything other than to make sure that there aren't any victims that still need assistance?

Trooper 2: Right. The common procedure is to secure the scene and wait to preserve evidence, but also use the crime lab, and we called the Detective Sergeant.

Prosecutor: And did the crime lab, in fact, come?

Trooper 2: Yes.

Prosecutor: And what was your participation after the crime lab got there? Did you participate in the search?

Trooper 2: I made entry well after the crime lab and the detective sergeants had arrived. Just some brief observations at the scene: I also wrote the search warrant for the residence and for the vehicle.

Prosecutor: And after you and Trooper 3 secured the scene, is that when you basically wrote the search warrant?

Trooper 2: Yes.

Prosecutor: Okay. And did you participate in the search for the vehicle at all?

Trooper 2: I did.

Prosecutor: And what can you tell me about that?

Trooper 2: We searched the vehicle at (REDACTED) towing it was, I believe, a few days after the accident: We did find a red cord which we believe came from the garage door at the house, and we also found a lamp that we believed was also related to the victim's house.

Judge: We're talking about the Tahoe?

Trooper 2: That's correct.

Prosecutor: And that green Tahoe that was towed to (REDACTED) as part of the securing of the evidence?

Trooper 2: Yes. It was secured in his enclosed facility there.

Prosecutor: So that nobody would have access to that until a search warrant could be executed?

Trooper 2: That was the understanding, yes.

Prosecutor: And why did you believe that a lamp you found may have been used – I'm sorry, may have been part of this incident?

Trooper 2: I believe it's, just from the ongoing investigation, possible. I can't speak to the interviews there, but through working with the detective sergeants, it was believed that that was tied there as well.

Judge: Did you see anything unusual with the lamp when you seized it?

Trooper 2: After referring to my report here, I believe it's not a lamp, it's a furniture leg, and it had blood spatter – appeared to have blood spatter on it.

Prosecutor: And by furniture leg, do you know, was it a table leg, or a chair leg, or do you know what kind of leg that would have been?

Trooper 2: I don't recall at this time.

Judge: And there was an orange cord - Trooper 2, I have some privy to your report. The attorneys stipulated to allow me to review at least a portion of it. Is the cord believed to have been part of the garage door opener?

Trooper 2: Yes, Your Honor.

Prosecutor: And did you find anything by way of sleeping materials, anything like that in the vehicle?

Trooper 2: Yes, we found a sleeping bag.

Prosecutor: Did you find any business cards in there?

Trooper 2: Yes, we found a business card to (REDACTED), a psychologist from (REDACTED).

Prosecutor: And do you know, was that an appointment card or a reminder card?

Trooper 2: It was an appointment card for January 19th, 2021.

Judge: Did it show who the appointment was for?

Trooper 2: I don't believe so.

Prosecutor: May I approach the witness? Trooper 2, I've handed you what has been previously marked as Proposed Exhibits 2 through 6: Can you please take a look at each of those exhibits and tell me, when you're finished, if you recognize those?

Trooper 2: Yes.

Prosecutor: Okay. So, if you could start, Trooper 2, with exhibit number 2, if you could tell the court what that is and what you recognize there.

Trooper 2: It appears to be the entry door coming from the garage into the house.

Prosecutor: And is there a notable amount of blood all over the place?

Trooper 2: Yes.

Prosecutor: And potentially a pair of – it looks like scissors on the floor?

Trooper 2: Yes.

Prosecutor: And is that a fair and accurate depiction of how that entryway looked on the morning of March 17th, 2021, when you entered that residence?

Trooper 2: Yes, except for the door, I think is concealing even more blood behind the wall.

Prosecutor: Okay. So there's even more blood behind the wall?

Trooper 2: That's what I recall.

Prosecutor: But the view from that photograph itself, if you were standing in that position, that would be an accurate representation?

Trooper 2: Yes.

Prosecutor: Your Honor, at this time, I would move to admit People's proposed exhibit number 2 into evidence.

Judge: Exhibit 2 is received. Is there going to be an objection to any of them?

Defense Council: No, Your Honor.

Judge: Okay. People's exhibits 2 through 6 are received without objection.

Prosecutor: Now, Trooper 2, as far as Photograph number 3 or exhibit number 3, can you tell me what that depicts?

Trooper 2: This is the second bedroom where we found the first dead dog.

Prosecutor: And so that was the dog on the main floor?

Trooper 2: That's correct.

Prosecutor: And at that time, did you – were you able to note anything on that dog about that dog's injuries or apparent injuries to you?

Trooper 2: I believe I recall some – it looked like possible stab wounds.

Prosecutor: To that dog as well?

Trooper 2: Yes.

Prosecutor: Okay. Now, if you could turn your attention to exhibit number 4, can you tell me what that depicts?

MY FATHER'S STORY

Trooper 2: It's a photo of the victim.

Prosecutor: And is that – does that photo accurately represent how he – how you viewed him or how he was positioned when you arrived in that residence?

Trooper 2: Yes.

Prosecutor: Okay. And is there a firearm depicted anywhere in that photo?

Trooper 2: Yes.

Prosecutor: And where is the firearm?

Trooper 2: The firearm is lying on his left side.

Prosecutor: Okay. Now, if you could turn your attention to exhibit Number 5, can you tell me what that is, please?

Trooper 2: It's another photo, more of the room, but also includes the victim, and there appears to be some blood on the wall.

Prosecutor: Okay. And does that photo depict... are you able to see where the stairs are in that photo?

Trooper 2: Yes.

Prosecutor: In relation to the victim?

Trooper 2: Yes.

Prosecutor: And Photo Number 6, exhibit number 6, could you please identify that?

Trooper 2: That's an overall photo of the living room, which was also tied to the kitchen and generally close to where the victim was found.

Prosecutor: In that number 6, does that photo depict the kind of representation of how the residence appeared as far as in shamble at that point?

Trooper 2: Yes.

Prosecutor: And Trooper 2, you've entered lots of homes in your career as a trooper, correct?

Trooper 2: Yes.

Prosecutor: Can you tell- generally tell if a home is neatly kept or if it's not neatly kept?

Trooper 2: Yes.

Prosecutor: And in regard to this home can you tell me, do you believe that this home was neatly kept or was it messy?

Trooper 2: It seemed to be more neatly kept. This stood out to me as something that had – my impression was that it was in disarray due to a struggle and not due to someone just living in disarray.

Prosecutor: And you had previously testified that when you and Trooper 3 first came in, there was a wallet open in the middle of the hallway with an identification.

Trooper 2: Yes.

Prosecutor: Did you ever stop to take a look at that identification to see who it belonged to?

Trooper 2: I believe I took a closer look at it. We didn't want to disturb anything at that time, so I took a look, but then we backed out.

Prosecutor: Were you able to see who it belonged to?

Trooper 2: I don't recall looking that closely, honestly.

Prosecutor: Because you were not collecting evidence at this point?

Trooper 2: Not at that point, no.

Prosecutor: And I would assume that you'd know all that evidence would have been collected eventually, and it would be documented.

Trooper 2: Yes.

Prosecutor: Thank you. I don't have any further questions about this witness.

Defense Council: No questions, Your Honor.

Judge: Trooper 2, you're excused from your subpoena, sir, and please don't talk about your testimony with any other potential witnesses.

Chapter 14: Trooper 3

Prosecutor: Your Honor, I would call Trooper 3.

Clerk: Would you please raise your right hand? You solemnly swear or affirm that the testimony you give in the case will be the truth, the whole truth, and nothing but the truth, so help you God.

Trooper 3: I do.

Prosecutor: Good morning, Trooper 3. Could you please state and spell your name for the record?

Trooper 3: I'm Trooper (REDACTED).

Prosecutor: And sir, what is your occupation, for whom do you work?

Trooper 3: I'm a trooper with the Michigan State Police.

Prosecutor: Okay. Were you working on March 17th, 2021, around 8:00 a.m.?

Trooper 3: Yes, I was.

Prosecutor: And did something happen at that time?

Trooper 3: Yes, I was dispatched out to (REDACTED) for a well-being check.

Prosecutor: And when you got to that residence, what did you find?

Trooper 3: Well, initially, we were dispatched to the well-being check, got there, and the residence had an open door, the garage door was open, the attached garage, so we walked in, and through our investigation, we observed blood on the door in the garage with the main door being open in the residence.

Prosecutor: And is this just basically - at this point when you see that are you inclined to do a sweep of the residence than to make sure that there's nobody that's injured inside or anything?

Trooper 3: Yes. In this particular case, we were dispatched to the well-being check because we had information through Dispatch from EMS on a traffic crash that a subject had killed her boyfriend. This was what we were being told in that residence.

Prosecutor: And so you see blood in the entryway, what do you do next?

Trooper 3: Well, initially, after seeing the blood, we checked around the house to look for another way in, hoping we wouldn't have to go through all this blood, but we were not able to gain entry. We did find a double door, a French door, something along those lines with the screens drawn or the blinds drawn. I'm sorry, we were not able to see inside the residence. The doors were locked, and we weren't able to get in through that entry, so we had to come back through the garage. While looking around the exterior of the residence for another entry, we did observe what we believed was a bullet hole in a glass window pane above the doors.

Prosecutor: And that was before entering the residence?

Trooper 3: Correct.

Prosecutor: And so what happened when you entered the residence?

Trooper 3: Well, we, Trooper 2, and I entered the residence and started tactically making our way through clearing rooms as we went. I went into the first bedroom, which was closest to the door, and did not observe any significant issue there. In the next bedroom we went, we found a dead dog next to the bed. Then we continued through the residence, which goes into the kitchen area, and there we observed, of course, the whole way through, we're seeing blood all over walls, floors, doors, everything. Get into the kitchen, and from there, you can see the - I'll call it the living room of the house, just in total disarray: tables, chairs knocked over, blood, broken items all over. We observed a handgun on the counter of the kitchen, continued in through there, and that's where we located the deceased, at the bottom of the stairwell in the living room.

Prosecutor: Okay. And at that point, you located the deceased, you were aware right away that this individual was deceased, and there would be no way to render EMS at that point?

Trooper 3: Yeah. We did not attempt any lifesaving efforts. My partner, who was previously was an EMT, much more qualified in medical than I am, but it was very obvious that he was deceased. The smell in the room, it's very hard to describe, but the blood has a smell to it, something that I've experienced over 21 years of being a police officer, that whether it's at crash scenes or, you know, it's just a smell that's older, just a well-established smell in the residence. And I know Trooper 2 — well, Trooper 2 checked for vitals.

Prosecutor: And so you had indicated there was a firearm that you had found on the counter. Did you locate any other firearms at that point?

Trooper 3: Yes. There was also a pistol located next to his body.

Prosecutor: And then the firearm that was on the counter was a pistol as well?

Trooper 3: Yes.

Prosecutor: What did you do then?

Trooper 3: We continued our search of the residence, meaning the upstairs loft, we did an initial quick search. Well, when we went up to the loft, we did discover another dead dog, and then we also saw a knife on the bed, and, again, a lot of blood throughout the upstairs area.

Prosecutor: And the upstairs area is laid out how? Is it one big bedroom the upstairs leads to?

Trooper 3: Yes, and there's a bathroom attached to it, I believe.

Prosecutor: Okay, so the only place to go upstairs would be the bedroom and the attached bathroom?

Trooper 3: Yeah. I think there was a closet too, but I don't recall for sure.

Prosecutor: Now, you indicated that there was a dead dog upstairs: Did the dog appear to be – have died because of injuries, or were you able to tell whether it had trauma or anything?

Trooper 3: It was very apparent that – I believed they were gunshot wounds, I was wrong apparently, but yes, they were – there were injury wounds to the torso of both dogs.

Prosecutor: And once you determined.. were you able to determine whether there was anyone else in the residence? There was nobody else in the residence?

Trooper 3: Yea, we did confirm there was no one else in the residence:

Prosecutor: So what did you do then?

Trooper 3: Well, I guess we continued our way back out of the residence doing a more thorough search, checking closets, bathrooms, again everything just to double check, and then we exited the house, and I called the detective, Detective Sergeant 2.

Prosecutor: Now you – when you were engaging in this search, did you – or I'm sorry, just the sweep, I guess is a different term than search, but a sweep of the residence, did you ever notice a wallet or ID anywhere?

Trooper 3: Yes, we did, I Believe it was on the floor, and I don't remember, right by the kitchen area, might have been on a countertop.

Prosecutor: Were you able to observe that, or did you look at that time?

Trooper 3: I don't think I did. I don't recall doing that.

Prosecutor: Okay. Now after you secured the residence, what did you do regarding the investigation?

Trooper 3: I maintained a parameter, securing the scene outside until the detective team arrived.

Prosecutor: Okay. And once the detective team arrived, did they arrive in conjunction with the crime scene response team, or were they at a different time?

Trooper 3: Most of the detectives were before the crime lab was there, yes.

Prosecutor: Okay, and did you ever locate any evidence outside of the home?

Trooper 3: Yes, in searching the interior of the home, I observed a bullet hole in the, I'll call it a banister from the upstairs, and that bullet hole in the banister appeared to line up with the bullet hole in the glass that we had seen from the outside. And looking and just following the line while outside with the K-9 unit, we were looking around, and we discovered damage to a tree branch that, just from my life of hunting, believed to be from a bullet hole or a bullet, and another trooper and I went over and pulled the branch down to get a better look, and we could see what appeared to be the bullet, a bullet had lodged in that branch.

Prosecutor: And you guys kind of located – did you locate it in conjunction with one another?

Trooper 3: Yeah. We were just walking around looking a little bit on the exterior looking for that because I remember, you know, the trajectory of the bullet, and he and I went over, and I was showing him what I saw was the damage, and he pulled the branch down to look at it.

Prosecutor: May I approach, Trooper 3 I've handed you what's previously been marked People's proposed exhibit 18. Do you recognize that?

Trooper 3: Yes, I do.

Prosecutor: And what is that?

Trooper 3: It's the bullet hole in the window looking from the exterior, outside of the building.

Prosecutor: And how high up would you say that is?

Trooper 3: Nine to ten feet, I would say.

Prosecutor: And the bullet that you found that you believe to be on the same trajectory, how high off the ground was the branch?

Trooper 3: Seven feet, I guess, seven to eight feet.

Prosecutor: And would that say anything to you about a trajectory?

Trooper 3: It was on a downward angle from the loft through the window into the tree.

Prosecutor: And help me understand the bullet hole in the drywall: Where was that in conjunction with the bullet hole that's in the window?

Trooper 3: It was higher. I called it a banister, but yes, it's a drywall partition preventing someone from stepping over and crashing into the lower level.

Prosecutor: I see.

Trooper 3: So, it was higher, again, in trajectory from the window to the wall.

MY FATHER'S STORY

Prosecutor: Could I approach?

Judge: Yes, is 18 offered, Mr. Prosecutor?

Prosecutor: Yes.

Judge: People's 18 is received.

Prosecutor: Trooper 3, I've handed you People's Proposed 17 and 15, you could look at Proposed 17 first and tell me if you recognize that.

Trooper 3: Yes, I do.

Prosecutor: What is People's proposed 17?

Trooper 3: It's the bullet hole in the drywall. From the lower level, looking up is what you're seeing.

Prosecutor: And that is the banister that you had described?

Trooper 3: Yes.

Prosecutor: And that bullet hole is higher than the bullet hole that's in the glass in the previous exhibit?

Trooper 3: Yes.

Prosecutor: I would move to have people's proposed 17 admitted into evidence.

Judge: 17 is received.

Prosecutor: And Trooper 3, you could take a look at exhibit number – People's proposed exhibit number 15 and tell me if you recognize that.

Trooper 3: Yes, I do.

Prosecutor: And can you tell me what that is?

Trooper 3: That is the dog upstairs.

Prosecutor: Okay. And does that depict injuries to the body of the dog?

Trooper 3: Yes, it does.

Prosecutor: I would move to admit People's proposed exhibit 15 into evidence.

Judge: People's 15 is received.

Prosecutor: Thank you. Trooper 3, once you had found the bullet hole in the tree branch, did you do anything else regarding this incident?

Trooper 3: I stayed on scene to offer any assistance, but no, I did not do much.

Prosecutor: Okay. Thank you. I don't believe I have any further questions about this witness.

Defense Council: I have no questions, thank you.

Judge: Thank you, Trooper 3. Witness excused.

Chapter 15: Forensic Scientist 1

Prosecutor: Your Honor, I would call Forensic Scientist 1 to the stand.

Clerk: Would you please raise your right hand? Do you solemnly swear or affirm that the testimony you give in this case will be the truth, the whole truth, and nothing but the truth, so help you God?

Forensic Scientist 1: Yes, I do.

Judge: Right over here, Ms. Forensic Scientist 1. Good Morning.

Prosecutor: Good Morning, Ms. Forensic Scientist 1. Could you please state and spell your name for the record?

Forensic Scientist 1: Yes, it is (REDACTED).

Prosecutor: And, ma'am, what is your occupation? For whom do you work?

Forensic Scientist 1: I'm a forensic scientist with the Michigan State Police at the Marquette Forensic Laboratory.

Prosecutor: And how long have you been employed as a forensic scientist with the Michigan State Police?

Forensic Scientist 1: I've been employed for approximately six years.

Prosecutor 1: And how long have you been at the Marquette laboratory?

Forensic Scientist 1: I've been at the Marquette lab for six months. Before that, I was at Grayling for three and a half years.

Prosecutor: Okay. Were you assigned somewhere else before that?

Forensic Scientist 1: Yes. Then I was at the Metro Detroit lab for a year and a half.

Prosecutor: And do you have a specialty as a forensic scientist with the MSP?

Forensic Scientist 1: Yes. Currently, I'm in the controlled substances unit at the Marquette lab; while in Grayling and Metro Detroit, I was in the firearm and tool mark identification unit.

Prosecutor: And is it common in your profession to visit crime scenes?

Forensic Scientist 1: Yes, it is.

Prosecutor: And to, for lack of a better term, process those crime scenes?

MY FATHER'S STORY

Forensic Scientist 1: Yes.

Prosecutor: And did you process a crime scene on March 17th, 2021, in (REDACTED), Michigan?

Forensic Scientist 1: Yes, I did.

Prosecutor: What can you tell me about that?

Forensic Scientist 1: So when we arrived at the scene, we met with the officers that responded. They told us that there was a deceased male and two dead dogs inside. So I was the photographer for the scene, so I would have put on protective equipment, went in, and photographed the scene as we found it, and then I came outside and told my team what I saw. Again, there was a deceased male and two dead dogs.

Prosecutor: Okay, so would the first step that's done when the crime scene responds be that the photographer goes in and preserves everything photographically before things can be moved?

Forensic Scientist 1: Yes.

Prosecutor: Okay. And once you did that, what happened? Once you photograph the things that you need to photograph, what happens then?

Forensic Scientist 1: I would go to my team, and we would split up our different duties: So we have somebody else that's sketching the scene, and then we'll be doing evidence collection and taking notes of what's going on on the scene.

Prosecutor: And did you participate in the evidence collection?

Forensic Scientist 1: Yes, I did.

Prosecutor: Okay. And was there a certain type of evidence that you were looking for as opposed to maybe one of the other - maybe Mr. Forensic Scientist 2, one of the other scientists would be collecting, or how does it work?

Forensic Scientist 1: So we work as a team to find that evidence, identify what we deem as important, and so we mark all that and then take photos, and then we collect it. As to who's collecting it, it's just – so I was in firearms, so any firearms evidence I tried to collect that and make those firearms safe, so that was my job there.

Prosecutor: And as a result of, basically, your processing the scene, did you locate any firearms or any firearm-related evidence?

Forensic Scientist 1: Yes, I did.

Prosecutor: And what did you locate?

Forensic Scientist 1: I located three firearms and a fired cartridge case.

Prosecutor: Okay. Now, the firearms that you located, where were they located?

Forensic Scientist 1: There was one firearm, item L-1, which was located on the kitchen counter, there was another firearm, L-2, which was located near the victim, and there was another firearm located upstairs in the gun safe.

Prosecutor: So the firearm that was located upstairs was actually in the gun safe?

Forensic Scientist 1: Yes.

Prosecutor: Was the gun safe locked, or was it open?

Forensic Scientist 1: Yes, I believe we had to find a key and unlock that safe.

Prosecutor: And as far as pistol clips that would hold the rounds, did you locate any of those?

Forensic Scientist 1: Yes, there were several magazines with cartridges inside of them that were located around the scene. I believe in the living room, and I believe there were some upstairs also.

Prosecutor: And did you locate any cartridges, either loaded or empty, in the residence, and can you tell me where?

Forensic Scientist 1: Yes, there were several cartridges, meaning it still had the bullet in them, and it had not been fired, so there were several of those just scattered about the living room, and there was an emptied fired cartridge case, meaning it had been fired, and that was upstairs on the bed.

Prosecutor: And so we've already had – well, can you describe the upstairs of the residence?

Forensic Scientist 1: Yes. So upstairs was a bedroom and a bathroom: The bedroom had just the bed and some dressers, there was also a walk-in closet which is where the gun safe was, and there was also a deceased dog up there in the bedroom area.

Prosecutor: And you said that you found what you believed to be an empty cartridge up there?

Forensic Scientist 1: Yes, there was an empty fired cartridge case.

Prosecutor: And where was that cartridge case found?

Forensic Scientist 1: That was on the bed.

Prosecutor: Okay. Was there anything else on the bed with that cartridge case?

Forensic Scientist 1: Not that I recall. There may have been some blankets.

Prosecutor: Did you ever locate any knives in the residence?

MY FATHER'S STORY

Forensic Scientist 1: Yes. There was a pocket knife near the victim, and then there was also a large kitchen knife on the upstairs bed.

Prosecutor: That was on the upstairs bed?

Forensic Scientist 1: Yes.

Prosecutor 1: And would that have been the same bed as the spent cartridge was found?

Forensic Scientist: Yes.

Prosecutor: Forensic Scientist 1, I've handed you what has been marked People's proposed exhibits numbers 7, 10, 11, and 14. You could take me through each one of those individually, first starting with people's proposed exhibit number 7, and can you tell me if you recognize that and what that is, please?

Forensic Scientist 1: Yes. People's Proposed Exhibit number 7 is a .45 auto-caliber Smith & Wesson firearm.

Prosecutor: Okay. And where was that found?

Forensic Scientist 1: That was found on the kitchen counter.

Prosecutor: Okay, if you could turn your attention to People's 10, please.

Forensic Scientist 1: People's Exhibit number 11 also has another magazine with a cartridge in it which was also on the living room floor.

Prosecutor: And finally, People's 14.

Forensic Scientist 1: People's exhibit 14 has a kitchen knife that was located in the bedroom, on the bed in the upstairs bedroom.

Judge: Did you determine what caliber the cartridges were that were located in 10 and 11?

Forensic Scientist 1: I did not.

Prosecutor: Are People's 7, 10, 11, and 14 accurate representations of what they depict: That is, is that how those things appeared on that day when you took the photographs?

Forensic Scientist 1: Yes.

Prosecutor: Your Honor, at this time, I would move to admit People's Proposed 7, 10, 11, and 14 into evidence.

Judge: People's Exhibits 7, 10, 11, and 14 are received without objection.

Prosecutor: As regards the picture, I believe it's people's 7, is there, does there appear to be anything on that firearm?

MY FATHER'S STORY

Forensic Scientist 1: There is some red-brown staining on this firearm.

Prosecutor: Okay. And as regards the firearm that was found under the victim, do you know what type of weapon that was and what caliber?

Forensic Scientist 1: So that was a .45 Auto caliber Glock Model 21.

Judge: So they were both .45s?

Forensic Scientist 1: That's correct.

Prosecutor: And you don't know whether any of the - either the ammunition or the rounds were .45 necessarily?

Forensic Scientist 1: The fired cartridge case, the empty one that was on the bed, was .45 Auto caliber.

Prosecutor: AS far as .. as far as the magazines that are on the floor, we don't know necessarily what caliber those are?

Forensic Scientist 1: The ones in the magazines from People's Exhibit 11 and 10, I do not know if those are .45 Auto, but the loose cartridges that were strewn about in the living room were .45 Auto.

Judge: Did either of the handguns contain a magazine, if you know?

Forensic Scientist 1: Yes. So People's Exhibit 7, which is L·1, did have a magazine in it which had cartridges, and I do not know about L·2, the one that was under the victim. I'm not sure.

Prosecutor: You wouldn't have made a note of that or noted that in your records?

Forensic Scientist 1: The note that I have from that was there was no cartridge in the chamber, but I'm not sure if there was.

Prosecutor: If there was a photograph taken of that, would you be able to tell from that photograph?

Forensic Scientist 1: I might be able to.

Prosecutor: Your Honor, I believe that's People's 4. May I show that to the witness?

Judge: Yes.

Prosecutor: Forensic Scientist 1, I don't know if you'll be able to tell from that photograph or not, do you recognize People's 4?

Forensic Scientist 1: Yes, I do.

Prosecutor: Okay. And that's a photograph of the victim with the firearm near his body?

Forensic Scientist 1: Yes, it is.

MY FATHER'S STORY

Prosecutor: And can you tell me whether or not you can tell from that photograph whether that firearm had a magazine in it or not?

Forensic Scientist 1: I cannot tell from this photo if there was a magazine in there.

Prosecutor: Okay. That portion of the firemen would be blocked?

Forensic Scientist 1: Yes, it is.

Prosecutor: Thank you. Now, I want to ask you about any evidence of any fired rounds that you found in the home: Did you find any evidence of any fired rounds?

Forensic Scientist 1: We did find several bullet holes in the upstairs bedroom, like the one where the stairs go down. There was a bullet hole through there, and there was also an apparent bullet hole through the glass of the living room.

Judge: And then one empty shell casing?

Forensic Scientist 1: That's correct.

Prosecutor: I've handed you what has been marked as People's Proposed Exhibit 16: Can you tell me if you recognize that?

Forensic Scientist 1: Yes, I do.

Prosecutor: And what is that, please?

Forensic Scientist 1: People's Exhibit 16 shows bullet hole A-1, and this was in the one in the upstairs bedroom that led down the stairwell.

Prosecutor: So would that have kind of been - was there only one hole in the drywall?

Forensic Scientist 1: It would have come out - yes. There was another corresponding hole in the other side of the drywall.

Prosecutor: I would move to admit Exhibit 16 into evidence.

Judge: People's Exhibit 16 is received.

Prosecutor 1: Did you collect any other, say, blunt objects or anything that could have been used as a weapon?

Forensic Scientist 1: I collected pieces of a lamp that had red-brown staining on it.

Prosecutor: How many lamps did you collect? Did you collect more than one?

Forensic Scientist 1: I believe it was broken. It appeared to be like just broken pieces.

Prosecutor: And where were those located?

Forensic Scientist 1: Those were in the living room.

MY FATHER'S STORY

Prosecutor: Forensic Scientist 1, I've handed you what has been marked People's Proposed exhibits number 8 and 9. Do you recognize those?

Forensic Scientist 1: Yes, I do.

Prosecutor: Can you tell me first what 8 is and then what 9 is, please?

Forensic Scientist 1: People's Exhibit 8 is a lamp, yellow in color, and then People's Exhibit 9 is another piece of a separate lamp, so two separate lamps.

Prosecutor: And can you tell me exactly where each of those was found?

Forensic Scientist 1: People's Exhibit 8 was found in the living room near the victim. Then People's Exhibit 9 was found in the living room in the same general area near the victim.

Prosecutor: And do either of those Exhibits display any red-brown staining on either of the items?

Forensic Scientist 1: Yes, both of these, People's Exhibit 8 and People's Exhibit 9, do have red-brown staining on them.

Prosecutor: I would move to admit People's Proposed Exhibit Number 8 and People's Proposed Exhibit Number 9 into evidence at this time.

Defense Council: No objection.

ERIC JOHNSON

Judge: People's 8 and 9 are received.

Prosecutor: Ms. Forensic Scientist 1, as far as your role in this, you indicated you took photographs and you collected several items that we've already discussed: Did you do anything else regarding this incident?

Forensic Scientist 1: No, those were the only duties that I did at the scene.

Prosecutor: Okay, thank you. I don't have anything further.

Defense Council: No Questions, your Honor.

Judge: Thank you, Ms. Forensic Scientist. You're excused from your subpoena. If you could hand me the exhibits. Thank you.

Chapter 16: Forensic Scientist 2

Prosecutor: Your Honor, I would call Mr. Forensic Scientist 2 to the stand.

Clerk: Would you please raise your right hand? Do you solemnly swear or affirm that the testimony you give in this case will be the truth, the whole truth, and nothing but the truth, so help you God?

Forensic Scientist 2: Yes, I do.

Judge: Good Morning. Mr. Forensic Scientist, these are exhibits that are already in evidence. If you'd please place them on the bar, the attorneys may wish to refer to them.

Prosecutor: Good morning, Mr. Forensic Scientist 2. Could you please state and spell your name for the record?

Forensic Scientist 2: My name is (REDACTED).

Prosecutor: And sir, what is your occupation? For whom do you work?

Forensic Scientist 2: I am a forensic scientist. I'm the supervisor of the latent fingerprint unit at the Grayling Forensic Science Laboratory.

Prosecutor: And in that capacity, what kind of education and training do you have?

Forensic Scientist 2: I have a degree from (REDACTED) university in criminalistics with a minor in chemistry. For latent fingerprint work, I have been trained for two years as a latent fingerprint examiner to be able to do the job we're doing for crime scene investigation, and basically, our training is on the job, so that's - for the crime scene part of it, it's all on-the-job training.

Prosecutor: And how long have you been employed as a forensic scientist with the Michigan State Police Crime Lab?

Forensic Scientist 2: 27 years.

Prosecutor: And all that time have you spent at the Grayling Crime Lab, or have you been at other labs as well?

Forensic Scientist 2: Yes, I have. I also supervise the Marquette Latent Fingerprint unit, so I travel back and forth.

Prosecutor: And is it common to visit crime scenes in your line of work?

Forensic Scientist 2: Yes.

Prosecutor: And did you visit a crime scene on or about March 17th, 2021, in (REDACTED), Michigan?

Forensic Scientist 2: Yes, I did.

Prosecutor: What can you tell me about that?

MY FATHER'S STORY

Forensic Scientist 2: We were called in the morning to come to investigate a crime scene there, so we took the call, got our team together, and then made our way to the scene.

Prosecutor: And when you got to the scene, I assume there were already numerous detectives and uniformed officers on the scene?

Forensic Scientist 2: Yes, there were.

Prosecutor: Take me from you getting on the scene. What happened?

Forensic Scientist 2: We got some background information on what they thought they had, what was going on, so after that, I think we had the search warrant already, so after the search warrant was signed, our photographer goes around and does photography of the whole scene.

Prosecutor: And while the photographer is doing that, what do you do? Do you just wait?

Forensic Scientist 2: Just kind of waiting. We don't usually let anybody into the scene until the general photography is done so that everything is in place.

Prosecutor: And once the photography was done, you went into the residence?

Forensic Scientist 2: Yes. Then our team would walk through and go through and kind of see what are we dealing with.

Prosecutor: Okay. And you participated in that walk-through?

Forensic Scientist 2: Yes.

Prosecutor: What can you tell me about it?

Forensic Scientist 2: We entered through the garage and, you know, as soon as we walked in through the garage door into the residence, there was a lot of blood - apparent blood through the laundry room, carpets, walls, basically through the scene.

Prosecutor: And did it look like a struggle had taken place?

Forensic Scientist 2: Yes.

Prosecutor: And why do you say that?

Forensic Scientist 2: The two first bedrooms were neat and clean, and the master bedroom was neat and clean, but the main area down the great room, kitchen, everything was completely disheveled and looked like it was ransacked.

Prosecutor: And in the bedrooms, you described them as neat and clean, but was there anything of concern or note in any of those bedrooms?

Forensic Scientist 2: Yeah, in the second bedroom, there was a dead animal, a dead dog that appeared to be stabbed.

MY FATHER'S STORY

Prosecutor: Okay. And that would be the second bedroom on the first floor?

Forensic Scientist 2: Yes.

Prosecutor: What about the master bedroom upstairs?

Forensic Scientist 2: The master bedroom, of course, there was the victim at the bottom of the stairs, but there were blood trails all through the home, up the stairs, railings, and at the top - not the top of the stairs but into the master bedroom on the far wall there was another dead dog.

Prosecutor: And did that dog appear to have wounds as well?

Forensic Scientist 2: It was stabbed as well.

Prosecutor: Now, as it regards collection procedures, was there evidence that you collected as a result of this scene?

Forensic Scientist 2: Yes.

Prosecutor: What types of things were you looking for?

Forensic Scientist 2: We were looking for blood evidence, weapons, basically those were the main things.

Prosecutor: And you did find some weapons in the home?

Forensic Scientist 2: Yes.

Prosecutor: And those weapons were collected by Forensic Scientist 1?

Forensic Scientist 2: Yes.

Prosecutor: Did you collect any firearms?

Forensic Scientist 2: I'd have to look back at the evidence list, but I'm pretty sure I collected some of the gun magazines that were down in the main room.

Prosecutor: And those would have been on the main floor?

Forensic Scientist 2: Yes.

Prosecutor: And were those located near the victim?

Forensic Scientist 2: They were all strewn about all over the place.

Prosecutor: It is safe to say there were a number of those?

Forensic Scientist 2: Yes.

Prosecutor: What about cartridges? Did you find cartridges?

Forensic Scientist 2: We found single full cartridges strewn about upstairs and downstairs.

MY FATHER'S STORY

Prosecutor: Any spent cartridges?

Forensic Scientist 2: There was one spent cartridge. It was on the master bedroom bed.

Prosecutor: And did you observe any bullet holes anywhere in the residence?

Forensic Scientist 2: There appeared to be a bullet hole upstairs at the top of the master bedroom going from one side of the room to the other, through the railing, and appearing to go through the window.

Prosecutor: Mr. Forensic Scientist 2, I've handed you what has been marked People's Proposed Exhibits Number 12 and 13: Do you recognize those?

Forensic Scientist 2: Yes, I do.

Prosecutor: And can you tell me what each of those are, please?

Forensic Scientist 2: People's Proposed Exhibit Number 12 is a photograph of the stairway leading upstairs to the master bedroom, and the perspective is looking down the stairs. People's Proposed Exhibit 13 is the same shot, but It's just a little bit farther back, showing the railing and just a little bit of the master bedroom area.

Prosecutor: Is there anything notable about either of those photographs, particularly with the landing at the bottom of the stairs?

Forensic Scientist 2: Yes, at the bottom of the landing, there are blood stains.

Prosecutor: Okay, is that indicative of anything?

Forensic Scientist 2: It's indicative of someone bleeding in that area.

Prosecutor: Your Honor, at this time, I would move to admit People's Proposed Exhibits number 12 and 13.

Judge: People's Exhibits 12 and 13 are received.

Prosecutor: Now, regarding the blood that is not – depicted on the, I guess, the carpet of the landing, it appears that there's a lot of blood there, correct?

Forensic Scientist 2: It appears that way, yes.

Prosecutor: And you found blood throughout the residence?

Forensic Scientist 2: Yes.

Prosecutor: Was it smeared on the walls?

Forensic Scientist 2: It was, yes.

Prosecutor: Where else did you find it?

MY FATHER'S STORY

Forensic Scientist 2: There's a lot on the walls, on the railings, the carpet, the kitchen, it was all over the place, bathrooms as well.

Prosecutor: Thank you. I don't have anything further.

Defense Council: No questions, Your Honor.

Judge: Thank you, Forensic Scientist 2. You are excused.

Chapter 17: Trooper 4

Prosecutor: Your Honor, I would call Trooper 4 to the stand.

Clerk: Please raise your right hand. Do you solemnly swear or affirm that the testimony you give in this case will be the truth, the whole truth, and nothing but the truth, so help you God?

Trooper 4: I do.

Prosecutor: Good morning, Trooper 4. Please state and spell your name for the record.

Trooper 4: (REDACTED)

Prosecutor: And sir, what is your occupation? For whom do you work?

Trooper 4: I'm a State Police Trooper.

Prosecutor: And how long have you been employed in that capacity?

Trooper 4: As a trooper since 2000.

Prosecutor: I want to ask you about the morning of March 17th, 2021. On that date, did you have contact with someone named Angelee Ross?

MY FATHER'S STORY

Trooper 4: Yes, sir, I did.

Prosecutor: What can you tell me about that, and how did it come about?

Trooper 4: I was working on a large case from the day previously at our office at the prison, and a lot of my co-workers went out to respond to this incident. I was working on my case, so I stayed at the office. I'd later have a conversation with a trooper who had responded to the crash scene and found that Ms. Ross was transported by an ambulance by herself to the hospital. So we both decided it would be an outstanding idea for me to drop what I was doing immediately and head to the hospital just to be there for her. So I responded right to the hospital.

Prosecutor: And so your role in responding to the hospital was what exactly? Was it to perform an interview, or was it to babysit, for lack of a better term?

Trooper 4: Exactly right. I was supposed to be there just to keep an eye on Ms. Ross and make sure she didn't leave. We didn't want her there with a bunch of civilians, obviously, and I was told just to stand by, they were going to send someone right away to interview her.

Prosecutor: And so what part of the hospital was she at when you were there with her?

Trooper 4: I responded to the emergency room, and then I found her in one of the ER rooms.

Prosecutor: And did you wait there with her in the ER room?

Trooper 4: I did.

Prosecutor: And during your waiting with her, what can you tell me about her appearance?

Trooper 4: Right away, I was really shocked at her demeanor, not very typical of what you would run into in this situation: She was very euphoric, covered head-to-toe in blood, literally ingrained in her cuticles around her nails, and just very articulate and non-remorseful would be the best way to say it.

Prosecutor: Well, did she mention anything to you, or did she discuss anything with you?

Trooper 4: She did, quite a bit: In fact, right when I arrived, she noticed the state Police uniform, and she knew I was there because she had murdered her friend.

Prosecutor: And were these statements in response to any questioning by you?

Trooper 4: No, sir.

Prosecutor: Did you advise her of anything?

Trooper 4: I did. After about 10 - 15 minutes of being there, the ER staff had told me some of the things that had been going on. She was wandering around without any clothing on, so I thought it would be best to Mirandize her immediately, and I did that at roughly 09:30.

Prosecutor: And after having Mirandized her, did she indicate that she would speak to you?

Trooper 4: She did. In fact, because of the situation and the weirdness of everything, I read her each warning, which is unusual. I just made sure she understood it. She was very articulate.

Prosecutor: Did she indicate that she did?

Trooper 4: She did.

Prosecutor: And she indicated she was willing to speak to you?

Trooper 4: Yes, sir.

Prosecutor: And what did she tell you about this?

Trooper 4: You know, I just tried to get her to speak chronologically. I remember it was very, you know like she would jump around and talk about religion, but I got her to commit to somewhat of a chronological story to try to put it down as to what the heck happened. So basically, just starting, I refer to page 2 of my police report that you guys both have. Right away, you know, I noticed the blood on her. She was covered, completely naked sitting in the hospital. She wouldn't put the gown on, and the nurses would repeatedly try to get her to put the gown on, but she wouldn't.

Prosecutor: Okay.

Trooper 4: She would keep the door cracked and try to close it on me as if she wanted to do something with me, so I tried to keep opening the door and finally got her to just sit down and talk a little bit, and she had mentioned to me because God was on her side and she's a child of God, I told her that I'd agreed that she was a child of God and I just wanted to get to the truth of what had happened last night or early this morning.

Prosecutor: And what happened?

Trooper 4: Yeah, she stated that she and Bill lived together, she described it as a boyfriend/girlfriend relationship. She had mentioned to me that he used her for sex and cleaning purposes around the house, just kind of starting with some general talk there. I asked her to tell me what happened and how she ended up here, and she stated I killed Bill, his soul needed to be cleaned, he's a bad person, and I transcribed that immediately that day to my police report.

Trooper 4: I asked her what she meant by "needed to be cleaned", and she had kind of just closed her eyes and drifted offright back a little bit, and she didn't give me a direct answer at all. So immediately I'm trying to figure out, you know, put some rationale to this, I started asking her if she was using any sorts of narcotics, you know, what did you do, do you do any narcotics of any kind, and she had stated she does Meth and she would inject it into her body, and I remember her feeling very remorseful that she did that, and she stated she was upset because she disgraced her temple by shooting drugs into her system.

Trooper 4: Just to continue, she was not able to tell me exactly when she woke up, but when she did wake that morning, she stated she saw the light, kind of meaning like a religious belief she saw the light, and she described a gun locker that Bill had in his house or his closet area, she wasn't very sure about it, but she believed that it had some sort of lock on it. She remembered that Bill had called her, in quotes, "a bitch" and I had asked if they argued, if they were fighting, and she declined any type of argument at all, and she told me in the past, whenever they would argue Bill would hand her this gun, which is very strange, so I asked her a follow-up question, why in the world would he hand you a firearm, and she had responded that he trusted her and had no issues with her handling the gun, so that's how she gets the gun into her hand from their conversation together. When she received the firearm, she told me she realized he was not a good person and his soul needed to be cleaned, so she pulled the trigger and shot him.

Prosecutor: What did she say then?

Trooper 4: I inquired, did you hit him? She thought that she had struck him in the chest but was not sure. She wasn't sure if she hit him or not. She said that she had then kicked him, and he fell down the stairs. She was kind of describing this altercation on top of the stairway landing to the residence. So as he falls down the stairs, presumably getting injured, he is on the floor, and she proceeds to grab whatever she could to kill him. She told me she remembered grabbing a lamp or something similar and striking him in the head repeatedly, like in a bludgeoning fashion, she didn't know how many times. At some point, she had a knife in her hand, she wasn't able to tell me where she had obtained the knife from, and she thought that she struck him in his heart or chest area. And I had asked at that point if the shot she fired maybe had killed him, and she said, "No, he punched me in the head at some point during that altercation."

Trooper 4: She was not able to tell me how many times she shot or what type of handgun it was at all, and more or less was trying to put some rationale to this and figure out why on earth she would do this, and I asked her, in fact, why would she want to kill Bill, and she replied I did it for me, I did it to prove to God I'm worthy. And she kind of laid back again in the bed and just kind of closed her eyes. She kind of said some statements like "God loves me, I'll be forgiven, and she wanted to be pain-free with God." And just kind of getting into the history of the house a little more, I asked her if Bill was a narcotics user as well, and Ms. Ross stated that she had given Bill some Meth.

Trooper 4: I asked her how she gave him Meth, and she didn't respond. I asked this question several times in different fashions just to see if she was a narcotics user, if Bill was, and if she wasn't answering me. I asked her if Bill smoked Meth or injected it, and she just didn't answer. I was worried about her hurting other people, obviously, so I inquired as to, you know, if she had hurt anyone else, and that's when she stated, "I killed Bill's dogs as well" - which was pretty alarming. And she informed me she was not sure how she killed the dogs, but they needed to be sent to heaven as well, and she had killed them: She knew she had killed them because they weren't moving around. Just very, very strange.

Prosecutor: Okay. And she's kind of just going through and taking you through what happened, and you might interject with a question here and there, but this almost sounds like a narrative of kind of what happened?

Trooper 4: It was. I didn't have to ask a lot of questions. She was looking to talk at that point, I would say.

Prosecutor: Okay. At some point, did you get on the phone with somebody in her presence?

Trooper 4: I did. I believe - I had terrible phone reception, so they probably tried to call me a few times, but I finally was able to speak with our Detective Sergeant 2.

Prosecutor: And was Ms. Ross in a position to overhear any of that conversation?

Trooper 4: She was. I couldn't leave the room at all with what had happened, I wanted to stay right with her so she was within earshot for sure.

Prosecutor: And did the topic of self-defense ever come up?

Trooper 4: It did. I believe Detective Sergeant 2 asked me, "Do you think it was self-defense?" and I stated, "I don't believe it was self-defense." That's when Ms. Ross said, "Yes, yes, it was self-defense."

Prosecutor: Because she overheard you on the phone?

Trooper 4: Correct.

Prosecutor: And did you explore that further with her?

Trooper 4: I did. I wanted to figure out if they did have more of a fight or altercation, and right away, once I was off the telephone, she said, "No, no, it wasn't self-defense. I killed him."

Prosecutor: Did she say anything else when she said it wasn't self-defense, anything about being a victim, or his soul, anything like that?

Trooper 4: If I could, if you have page 3 of my police report, I don't believe there was anything, but I'd like to just double-check.

Prosecutor: And if you could take a look at your report, and when you're finished, if could you look at up at me.

Trooper 4: She did. She said, "It was not self-defense, I killed him, his soul needed to be cleaned, and I'm not a victim." These were all direct statements made by Ms. Ross.

Prosecutor: Did she indicate whether or not she had any injuries?

Trooper 4: She did not. In fact, I had looked for those, I saw some minor scratches, you know, but that was all consistent with what she was telling me.

Prosecutor: Anything else regarding drug use or anything like that? Did she make any other statements?

Trooper 4: No, no, and believe me, I was trying to put some rationale to this, and so I inquired and never got anywhere with that.

Prosecutor: Did you ask her if she shoots or smokes it?

Trooper 4: I did both of those, correct.

Prosecutor: And did she say she shot it?

Trooper 4: I'm looking through my report again, but I don't believe so. She stated initially, when I arrived and asked her right about Meth, she said she would inject it into her body, and that's when I had stated earlier she disgraced her temple by shooting drugs, she was pretty remorseful of that.

Prosecutor: Okay. When somebody injects a drug such as Methamphetamine, and they're a user of that drug, do they have, generally in your experience as a seasoned state

Police trooper, do they have marks on their body from that, either injection site or track marks? Did you notice anything like that on her body?

Trooper 4: No. I did go over as best I could with her short of an exam, I did look for those, and I didn't notice anything.

Prosecutor: And Trooper 4, do you see her here in the courtroom today?

Trooper 4: I do, seated at the defense table.

Prosecutor: Your Honor, please let the record reflect that the witness has identified the defendant.

Judge: It shall.

Prosecutor: And Trooper 4, as far as you testified as to a lot of specific things that were said, but just as far as her overall behavior and demeanor, how did it strike you?

Trooper 4: I've been in the state Police since '97 after I graduated high school basically, and certainly, no offense, ma'am, but just crazy, I have never seen anything like that before. Her demeanor was very non-remorseful, and I've investigated dozens Of homicides myself, and I've never run into that. And especially, like, I talk about being covered in blood, but you really have to see the images, but it was so ingrained into her cuticles, I hate to describe it this way, but if you're outside digging all day that's how much the blood was ingrained in her fingers and under her nails.

Prosecutor: Her facial area, was there blood as well?

Trooper 4: She did. She was covered from head-to-toe in blood, naked with blood pretty much everywhere.

Prosecutor: And you made a statement when you first started testifying about her refusing to cover up and wandering in the ER. What can you tell me about that?

Trooper 4: The nurses had told me they were very grateful that I arrived quickly because she was wandering in the ER, and of course, they've got everything from the elderly to babies in there, so they were grateful to get her contained in one room with me there. Just very erratic behavior, very euphoric at times. Yeah, to be honest with you, as a normal person, I think the best word to describe it is just crazy behavior.

Prosecutor: And did you attempt to get her to cover up?

Trooper 4: Numerous times, along with the nursing staff.

Prosecutor: And what was her response every time you tried to do that?

Trooper 4: Just would take, you know, just nonchalantly as you or I would take off our jackets, she would just drop her blanket off.

Prosecutor: And at any point during your kind of watching over her waiting for the interview, at any point were you uncomfortable with kind of what was going on?

Trooper 4: To be honest, the whole time. I was calling, trying to get a cell phone signal to get messages out to my boss to get a female officer there and some help because I was alone with a potential homicide suspect. Ms. Ross would routinely stare at my genital area, which was uncomfortable, and try to shut the door to the ER room as I tried to keep it open. The nurses were busy, but I tried to get them to stay in the room with me, and they wouldn't. It was just very strange.

Prosecutor: How long do you think that you were just alone?

Trooper 4: I know exactly how long I was there: I was there from 9:15 until, I believe it was 10:50 when my backup female officer arrived.

Prosecutor: And that would have been Detective Trooper 1?

Trooper 4: Correct.

Prosecutor: And was Trooper 5 there as well at that time?

Trooper 4: He did. I believe they were doubled up that day, so they both arrived.

MY FATHER'S STORY

Prosecutor: And when they got here, what did you do?

Trooper 4: I advised both of them of the situation. We were standing there watching her, we couldn't take eyes off of her, so they kind of knew what I had done and that I had Mirandized her at 9:30, and we'd been talking. They also had brought over a digital camera from the post, which was in cadillac, so they could take some crime scene photos of her, and then I believe she was scheduled at that time or roughly for a CT scan as well.

Prosecutor: Okay. And so, is that the extent of your participation, at least as in regards either interviewing the witnesses or doing any kind of investigation?

Trooper 4: Yes, sir, it was.

Prosecutor: Thank you. I don't have anything further.

Defense Council: No questions, Your Honor.

Judge: Thank you, Trooper 4.

Chapter 18: Detective Trooper 1

Prosecutor: Your Honor, I would call Detective Trooper 1.

Clerk: Would you please raise your right hand? Do you solemnly swear or affirm that the testimony you give in this case will be the truth, the whole truth, and nothing but the truth, so help you God?

Detective Trooper 1: Yes, I do.

Prosecutor: Good Afternoon, Detective Trooper 1. Could you please state and spell your name for the record?

Detective Trooper 1: I am Detective Trooper Specialist (REDACTED), Michigan State Police.

Prosecutor: And Detective Trooper 1, what is your occupation, for whom do you work?

Detective Trooper 1: I work for the Michigan State Police, I'm assigned to the marijuana and tobacco investigative section.

Prosecutor: And on March 17th, 2021, were you assigned as a trooper to road patrol?

Detective Trooper 1: Yes, sir, I was.

Prosecutor: And on that date, did you have contact with someone named Angelee Ross?

Detective Trooper 1: Yes, I did.

Prosecutor: And how did that contact come about?

Detective Trooper 1: That contact came about because we were requested. I was at the post taking care of another investigation, and I was requested specifically as a female officer to respond to the hospital here in Manistee to assist with a situation that they had there and to deal with a woman who was currently being treated in the emergency room.

Prosecutor: And before I get into too much of that, there is one thing I did want to ask you. Are you trained in recognizing potential drugs or a drug recognition expert? Do you have that training?

Detective Trooper 1: I do have that training.

Prosecutor: And what does that consist of?

Detective Trooper 1: A drug recognition expert is specifically trained by police officers in the State of Michigan, and actually throughout the United States, to recognize an individual who may be under the influence or impaired by one of seven different drug categories. We're trained in recognizing drug usage, what the individual may behave like when they are on a particular drug or several types of different drugs, and what that type of impairment may mean as far as their reactions or actions if they are speaking, walking, or driving a vehicle.

Prosecutor: And have you put that training into practice as a police trooper?

Detective Trooper 1: Yes, I have.

Prosecutor: And is there a certification process for that?

Detective Trooper 1: Yes, there is.

Prosecutor: And have you kept up that certification process?

Detective Trooper 1: I did. I am not currently certified because of my role, my current investigative role, but I had kept it up. Yes, I had been re-certified: I was certified in 2016.

Prosecutor: And how long did that certification last?

Detective Trooper 1: Two years.

Prosecutor: Now, you just haven't kept it up because you're not working in that capacity anymore?

Detective Trooper 1: That's correct.

Prosecutor: Okay, so you indicated you were at the post and you got called because they needed a female officer. You were at the post, would that have been in Cadillac?

Detective Trooper 1: Yes, sir, that's the Cadillac post.

Prosecutor: And you were called to go to Munson Manistee Hospital?

Detective Trooper 1: That's correct.

Prosecutor: Kindly tell me what happened and what you found when you arrived.

Detective Trooper 1: So we were requested to go over and assist with another trooper's investigation because there was a female who had been in a situation, as far as I knew, she had been in a traffic crash, and when they checked on another individual that lived with her, they found that individual deceased. They weren't quite certain what they had, so they requested that I respond over there to be with the female individual.

Prosecutor: And where did you meet with her?

Detective Trooper 1: We met with her in the emergency room: She was in a private room just behind the emergency room desk where the nurses are.

Prosecutor: And when you went into the room to meet with her, was anybody else in there?

Detective Trooper 1: Trooper 4 was there, Michigan State Police, he was part of my squad at that time, and he stepped out of the room and briefed us just very briefly, but he had spoken with her and that she had been Mirandized by him and she was talking with him, and she seemed to be cooperative at the time.

Prosecutor: And you said "us", Was there another trooper that was there?

Detective Trooper 1: Yes, there was my partner, yes.

Prosecutor: And that would have been who?

Detective Trooper 1: Trooper 5.

Prosecutor: And were you doubled up that day, that is, two people in one car or did you have multiple cars?

Detective Trooper 1: We were doubled up that day, two people in one car.

Prosecutor: So once you met with Trooper 4, did you meet with Ms. Ross?

Detective Trooper 1: I did meet with her, yes.

Prosecutor: What was your initial impression? Tell me about that.

Detective Trooper 1: So when we were first getting there, we had heard that she was involved in a crash and that she was covered in blood, and information was coming out, we just didn't have a lot, so I expected to see, when I walked into the room, a woman covered in blood, I expected to see fresh blood on her and someone that may have been traumatized, or excited, or crying, or hysterical. I was anticipating that type of behavior, and when I walked in, I remember specifically that the blood that I saw was on her face and her body, but it wasn't wet blood, it was dried blood, and it appeared it had been there for a while, and she appeared to be very calm, almost relaxed. Some people get excited when a uniformed presence comes into the room; she did not get excited or anxious; she just appeared to be very calm, as a matter of fact.

Prosecutor: And when you entered the room, what was she wearing?

Detective Trooper 1: She was wearing a hospital gown, and she was covered in hospital blankets.

Prosecutor: And did you begin speaking with her right away?

Detective Trooper 1: I did. We introduced ourselves just to try and build a rapport with her and put her at ease, which she was mostly at ease. And just told her who we were and why we were there to check on her.

Prosecutor: And did she appear to be agreeable to speaking with you?

Detective Trooper 1: She did, yes.

Prosecutor: Tell me about the conversation, what happened?

Detective Trooper 1: So when we first walked in and after I introduced myself and Trooper 5, one of the first things that she said was, "I'm not worthy, I'm not worthy," and I didn't quite understand what that meant, but we just continued to talk with her and tried to put her at ease, and we just told her that we were there to check on her and make sure she was okay.

Prosecutor: And how did she respond to that?

Detective Trooper 1: She seemed to be okay with that. She just kept saying that she wasn't worthy, and she seemed to be, like I said before, I guess the best way to describe it is just rather matter-of-fact, kind of casual at that time.

Prosecutor: And how long did that go on? That exchange where she says, "I'm not worthy."

Detective Trooper 1: That went on for a little bit until it was time for her to go for a CT scan, and then because of the traffic crash, it was part of her treatment, she was reluctant to go and have that procedure done, she stated she didn't want any more radiation into her body, but the nurses talked to her, and I talked with her for some time to make sure that she could get checked out to make sure she was okay, then she complied.

Prosecutor: And so, did she leave the room for a while?

Detective Trooper 1: She did, but I went with her, and we were in the room when she got the CT scan, and then I accompanied her back to the examining room.

Prosecutor: And when you got back to the examining room, did you resume the conversation?

Detective Trooper 1: I did.

Prosecutor: And what can you tell me about that?

Detective Trooper 1: I asked if she took any medications. I was concerned that she was so calm that she had been given some medication or perhaps she needed her medication. She takes a normal medication, I just wanted to make sure she was in her normal state at that time.

Prosecutor: And what did she tell you?

Detective Trooper 1: She told me she took Methamphetamine.

Prosecutor: And how did you respond to that?

Detective Trooper 1: I said, "Do you mind if I look at your hands and your arms?" And she said, "That's fine." I noticed that her teeth were fine, so I surmised that I wanted to look for a different route of ingestion 17 Of the Methamphetamine as opposed to smoking.

Prosecutor: Because if someone smokes Methamphetamine, in your experience and training and knowledge, what happens?

Detective Trooper 1: Generally, you see some decay and some rot in their teeth, or some type of discoloration around their face and their nose, and their fingertips usually have some type of brown tar-type residue.

Prosecutor: What would be another method of ingesting Methamphetamine?

Detective Trooper 1: Injection.

Prosecutor: Okay. And so when somebody injects Methamphetamine, are there symptoms that you can look for on that person's body?

Detective Trooper 1: You can, yes. You can see basically what is called track marks or injection sites. So from my experience and training, I know that women primarily inject either in their fingers, between their fingers, or in their toes primarily. Sometimes there are some in their hands, and sometimes they are in their neck.

Prosecutor: And did you look for those signs on the body of Ms. Ross?

Detective Trooper 1: Yes, I did. I asked if I could look, and she said that was fine, so I did look at her hands, her arms, and her neck.

Prosecutor: And did you note or notice any sign of Methamphetamine use anywhere on her body?

Detective Trooper 1: I did not notice any type of injection sites.

Prosecutor: Okay. Did you ever ask her - well, let me ask you this, did she mention anything else about Methamphetamine in pill form or anything like that?

Detective Trooper 1: So when I was looking at her neck, I had gotten up to the point of her neck, and she did mention that - and I asked her how much she takes, and she said she takes it every day, and then it was about this point in our conversation the she let me know that she takes it in pill form, and when I asked more about that, like, okay, tell me about that, she said it was Adderall that she takes.

Prosecutor: Okay, so she said that she took Methamphetamine in pill form, but then said it was Adderall that she takes?

Detective Trooper 1: That is correct.

Prosecutor: And she takes it every day?

Detective Trooper 1: Yes.

Prosecutor: Now can you continue with the rest basically of the interaction with Ms. Ross: Where did it go from there once you were able to determine whether she was under the influence of anything at that point?

Detective Trooper 1: I was not able to determine if she was under the influence of anything at that time.

Prosecutor: And so - so you proceeded with an interview at that point?

Detective Trooper 1: We did. We continued to talk with her just to try and keep her calm and just build a rapport with her, let her know that we were there to check on her and make sure she was okay. We discussed a lot of the marks on her hands: I know she had significant marks, they were fresh bruises and swelling on her right hand, and then I noticed, which was very – I thought very remarkable, was the dried blood in her fingertips, and what I mean by the blood in her fingertips, it was in her fingernails and it was... it was deeply embedded almost like the best example I could give is if someone was gardening and you were digging in your yard, and you were done, and all that dirt is underneath your fingernails, and it's on top of your fingernails, that's what I noticed on her hands, and it was quite a bit, and it was dried blood.

Prosecutor: Would that be unusual to you in someone who has been involved in a murder scene?

Detective Trooper 1: Unusual to me for someone who's been involved in a murder scene?

Prosecutor: Yes. If you had seen that - I mean, have you seen that before in your experience?

Detective Trooper 1: I have not seen that much dried blood on the hands before, no, and I was informed that she was involved in a motor vehicle crash and that she was covered in blood, so I've not seen that type of marks or red blood on someone who was involved in a motor vehicle crash like that.

MY FATHER'S STORY

Prosecutor: Okay. So, what happened then?

Detective Trooper 1: So we continued to talk about her hands and the blood, and she had blood on her face, and I asked her about the blood on her face, and she said, "It's not mine." I said, "Well, whose is it?" and she said, "It's Bill's." I asked her about blood anywhere else, and she told me it was Bill's, it wasn't hers.

Prosecutor: And did you ask her any more about that?

Detective Trooper 1: I did. I asked her to tell me about it, you know, "Where is Bill? Do I need to check on him? Is he okay with the amount of blood you have on yourself?" And she told me, "I killed Bill, he's gone, he's dust."

Prosecutor: How did she say it?

Detective Trooper 1: Just like I said it.

Prosecutor: Matter of fact?

Detective Trooper 1: Matter of fact.

Prosecutor: Did you detect any remorse or anything like that in the way it was said?

Detective Trooper 1: I did not detect any type of remorse. Her expression didn't change when she said it.

Prosecutor: And what did she say then?

Detective Trooper 1: I asked her to tell me more about it, and she would start talking about seeing lights and seeing red lights and green lights and seeing dust in the air, electricity, and when I asked her if the dust or the lights was actual dust, or if it was Angelee, or if it was Bill she got really quiet, she didn't want to talk too much more about that, and she started talking about other things not being real, and extra worldly things, and seeing lights and dust.

Prosecutor: Okay, you said she became quiet: Did her overall demeanor change when she became quiet?

Detective Trooper 1: Her body movements didn't change. She stayed covered up, and just kind of sat underneath her blankets, and her body and the inflection in her voice would change when she talked about otherworldly things, or when she talked about the lights, and when she talked about being angered and being so empowered and channeling her anger she's never felt that type of anger or energy before, and at one point she made a comment, I'd have to look exactly at my report to see what it was, but she said she's never felt that type of energy in her heart before, and wow, and she was just enthusiastic about making that accident.

Prosecutor: And so her demeanor became more animated, I guess, is that safe to say, when she was talking about those things, more excited?

Detective Trooper 1: Yes. She got more excited when she talked about those things.

Prosecutor: Because initially, it sounds like she almost had more of a flat affect, matter of fact, when she is talking about things?

Detective Trooper 1: She did.

Prosecutor: And so it was when she was talking about the energy coursing through her, flowing through her, that she became more excited?

Detective Trooper 1: She did. There was almost - it was almost like a smile on her face: It was almost like she was excited to share that with us.

Prosecutor: And how did you respond to that?

Detective Trooper 1: I just asked her to tell me more. I just listened to her and watched her intently because of her face. I wanted to watch her face specifically because I was looking at all of this blood, the change in her face, and the change in her tone and her demeanor.

Prosecutor: And when you asked her to tell you more, did she?

Detective Trooper 1: She did.

Prosecutor: What did she tell you?

Detective Trooper 1: She told me that, when I asked about Bill, if I specifically needed to go check on him, if he was okay, and she said no, he's dead, he's dust, and when we talked more about that she said that she had killed him, and then when I asked her to tell me more, what do you mean, what does that mean, she'd said at one point in our contact that she had taken a gun from upstairs and shot the gun and it missed Bill, but it somehow misfired, she was using the word misfired, and the energy channeled through her and there was a force, and at one point she saw an opportunity to push him down the stairs and she took that opportunity because the force was helping her and the energy was helping her, and she'd grabbed a lamp and she was having a hard time explaining if it was a clear lamp or if it was an orange lamp, but she remembered grabbing a lamp and hitting Bill with the lamp, and at one time she even said that when the gun had misfired she had taken the gun and she had hit him with the gun.

Prosecutor: And did she continue through that whole incident in resolving it? Did she indicate how it ended, or did she continue talking about that?

Detective Trooper 1: She would continue talking about it. We had contact with her for several hours, and she would go from talking about the energy and experience channeling her anger and channeling her energy and feelings. And then to being rather calm and stating, "This isn't real, I have to use the restroom, and I don't think that's real, so maybe I should just go right here," and we tell her, "No, wait a second, we'll find someone for you." But she doesn't listen and said, "But it's not real," and we said, "Yes, it is real, we're real, we're here."

Prosecutor: So did you take that to mean that none of you were real and the situation wasn't real in her eyes?

Detective Trooper 1: I wasn't exactly sure what she meant by what wasn't real, because there would be a time when she would say – it seemed to be very lucid in saying I killed Bill, and then the next minute, she was talking about extraterrestrial beings and forces, but it's not real, and I have to accept that. But – and then she would say, "But it is real, and I had to do it because he wasn't going to be saved and he had to love," and when I asked her where Bill was now, she said, "He's reincarnated now."

Prosecutor: So did she indicate any other reason why she had done what she had done to Bill to you other than just he's gone, he's got to the learn, I think you said?

Detective Trooper 1: She said he wasn't going to be – he wasn't chosen. She said she and he had talked and he wouldn't listen to her and he only accepted things as what they were at face value, and that the force or otherworldly beings helped her and told her that Bill wasn't going to be chosen and he wasn't going to be saved, so she had to save him by basically killing him.

Prosecutor: Okay. Did she indicate if she was ever upset that Bill didn't believe her about these things?

Detective Trooper 1: She did not indicate that she was upset. She just talked about how he wasn't going - he wasn't chosen. She said she'd gotten messages from the dogs at one time, the dogs were giving her signals that Bill wasn't chosen and that she would say something and the dogs would growl at a particular comment that she would make, so she interpreted that as Bill wasn't chosen and that she had to kill him.

Prosecutor: Did she say anything about the dogs?

Detective Trooper 1: She did eventually when Detective Sergeant 1 came, she talked about killing the dogs then.

Prosecutor: Okay. But that wasn't in your initial interview?

Detective Trooper 1: That was not in my initial interview, no.

Prosecutor: And at some point, Detective Sergeant 1 did come in and conduct an interview, is that correct?

Detective Trooper 1: That's correct.

Prosecutor: And you were present for that?

Detective Trooper 1: Yes, sir, I was.

Prosecutor: And you contributed to that interview or helped with that interview?

Detective Trooper 1: Yes, I helped with that interview.

Prosecutor: And why did you help with that interview?

Detective Trooper 1: When Detective Sergeant 1 arrived, Angelee didn't want to talk with him, and he spoke with her like we are speaking right now, and he introduced himself and told her that he was there to talk with her and wanted to read Miranda to her, and I remember him reading it to her, and I was doing something, I was caught up doing something standing by her bedside, I think I was on her right side, and I remember Detective Sergeant 1 saying, "Are you with me?" so I looked up to see what was going on at the moment and she just had a very blank stare like she was almost looking right through Detective Sergeant 1. So, she said she didn't understand, he started over again, and when I would talk to her, she would acknowledge me, so at this point, it's like she basically requested that I stand by her and put my hand on her shoulder and talk with her and at that time she felt more comfortable, I believe, speaking with Detective Sergeant 1 when I would put my hand on her shoulder.

Prosecutor: Did her demeanor change at all when Detective Sergeant 1 came into the room?

Detective Trooper 1: Yes.

Prosecutor: How so?

Detective Trooper 1: Like she just stopped, she stopped participating, like she just put up a wall and stopped talking.

Prosecutor: And had you developed a rapport with her before that? Had she been talking to you?

Detective Trooper 1: She was talking with me the entire time that I was there.

Prosecutor: What about Trooper 5?

Detective Trooper 1: She talked with him as well, she flirted with him as well, but she didn't talk with him; she talked more with me.

Prosecutor: And you said that when you first went into the room she had a hospital gown, she was wrapped up in blankets, did that continue throughout your interview with her?

Detective Trooper 1: It did not.

Prosecutor: Tell me about that.

Detective Trooper 1: I asked her if I could take some photographs Of her body because she'd said that Bill had attacked her, and then she would say I can't lie about that, so I wanted to take some photographs of her body to, in fact, see if he had attacked her, if she had injuries what type of injuries, and document what we saw and what she said. I asked Trooper 5 to step out of the room for modesty purposes, so it was just myself and Angelee in the examining room, and he stepped outside. He was right outside the door, I think we cracked the door just a little bit because he could hear me, and I could hear him, so we were within earshot.

Detective Trooper 1: So as I told her what I was going to do, I was going to take photographs and where I was going to take the photographs, and I specifically told her we would cover her up for modesty purposes. So, I said can you help me with this, and she helped me: She would pull her hair back, and then I would move her hair or her arm, and the more I would move her arm or her hair, or position myself for the photograph, the more she enjoyed it: She would moan or smile, and then she really - it's almost like she was finding pleasure in that moment and her demeanor changed: It changed from very flat to almost a sexual-type enjoyment where she began to just pull off her clothing, and she pulled off her gown and kicked off the blankets, and as quickly as I would grab the blanket and cover her up and try to take the photograph she was just as quickly grabbing my free arm and pulling the blankets down while I'm trying to snap the photograph.

Prosecutor: And you said that when you're snapping the photographs, it's almost pleasure, do you mean like sexual pleasure?

Detective Trooper 1: Yes.

Prosecutor: And what about that? You were gloved up, I assume?

Detective Trooper 1: Yes.

Prosecutor: And so when you attempted to cover her up at times, did your hand ever brush parts of her body, shoulder, anything or like that?

Detective Trooper 1: Her shoulder, yes. Her hair, yes. I'm certain that there was a time when I would move her hand or her arm so that I could get a position. I know she had an injury on the bottom of her arm and her forearm, and I wanted to take a picture of that: Those parts of her anatomy I did touch.

Prosecutor: And when you did that, was there a reaction from her?

Detective Trooper 1: She enjoyed it.

Prosecutor: How did that – how did you tell she enjoyed it? What was there – how did that manifest itself? What was her response?

Detective Trooper 1: She was moaning, and she made a comment, "Your touch feels so good."

Prosecutor: And at some point, Trooper 5 came back in the room, correct?

Detective Trooper 1: Yes.

MY FATHER'S STORY

Prosecutor: And why did Trooper 5 re-enter the room?

Detective Trooper 1: Because I summoned him back to the room: There was a point in our contact that I was feeling uncomfortable with her behavior: She was becoming more sexualized, and at this point, I didn't think this was a good environment for me to be in by myself because she was just not cooperating as far as I was taking photographs, and she had no clothing on by the time I'd finished taking her photographs, so I opened the door all the way and told Trooper 5 he needed to come into the room immediately.

Prosecutor: And he did, in fact, come into the room?

Detective Trooper 1: Yes.

Prosecutor: And once he came back in the room, did her demeanor change at all?

Detective Trooper 1: Not immediately, no. She maintained that state, she said she was comfortable being in that natural state, and we encouraged her multiple times to cover up with a blanket in case the door opened, to put her clothing back on, and she just refused. There was one point I thought I saw goosebumps on her arm, and we asked her if she was chilled and we just continued to suggest that she get dressed, and she did not.

Prosecutor: So that happens. How soon after you're done with the photos and Trooper 5 comes back in does Detective Sergeant 1 get on scene, how soon after?

Detective Trooper 1: It was a short time after, I think he arrived about 1:00, that's not a short time because we got there about 11:00, so we had contact talking with her for about two hours before Detective Sergeant 1 arrived.

Prosecutor: And in the photographs and Trooper 5 coming back into the room, is that late into your contact with her? Would you say that's shortly before Detective Sergeant 1 arrived?

Detective Trooper 1: That's correct, it would be shortly before Detective Sergeant 1 arrived.

Prosecutor: And so then you're present for the interview with Detective Sergeant 1 you already testified?

Detective Trooper 1: Yes.

Prosecutor: And after that interview, what happens?

Detective Trooper 1: After that interview, we took biological samples from her hair and her hands for a search warrant that Detective Sergeant 1 had obtained.

Prosecutor: And once you did that, at any point did you allow her to clean herself up or suggest that maybe she should do that?

Detective Trooper 1: I did. After we had taken the samples, we took photographs of her face before any type of cleaning up and before any samples, and we took the biological samples from her fingernails and her hair, I noticed that there was something in her hair and on the sides and also up the crown of her head she had something else in her hair, so after that we think Detective Sergeant 1 stepped out for a moment Just to take care of some paperwork and he came back in and we were going to package up the samples, and that's when I took the sterile water that he had brought to clean up her face.

Prosecutor: And did you clean up her face, or did she?

Detective Trooper 1: I did.

Prosecutor: What can you tell me about that?

Detective Trooper 1: So when I was looking at her complexion when we first got there and during our contact with her, she almost looked like she was tanned or had make-up on: Her skin looked like make-up, it was not pale, it just had a tanned tone to it. When I took the sterile water and put it on the paper towel because we were going to transport her to the jail and I took the paper towels and the sterile water, I told her it was going to be cold, and she said it was fine. And I started to wipe the blood – dried blood off her face, and she had dried blood on her nose and in her ear, and I started to wipe it off, and as I'm wiping it off, the paper towel is rust colored and her complexion is changing. So I continued to wipe her face off and once I got her face completely wiped off, her complex was pale, much like it is right now in the courtroom.

Prosecutor: And is it your belief that, based on everything that you had seen, what you are wiping off was blood?

Detective Trooper 1: Yes, it is.

Prosecutor: If that blood had been due to, say, a spattering effect, is that – is that what you witnessed that you were wiping off, or was it something else?

Detective Trooper 1: I didn't – I didn't see any type of blood spatter: It was a large portion of blood on her forehead, like a thicker portion of blood on her forehead, almost like a significant nosebleed where their blood came from the nose and then ran across the face, which I thought was unusual because usually with a blood nose it would run down, so it ran across her face. She had dried blood in her ear, and it was thick blood, not like it had been wiped away; but the rest of her face I couldn't – It didn't look like she had cried through it, it almost looked like a make-up application, like it (had) been smoothed.

Prosecutor: Like a foundation, like rubbed in?

Detective Trooper 1: Like a make-up foundation rubbed in almost, yes, rubbed in, smoothed across. I mean, there was a little bit of a marking on her forehead, but across her face and chin, it just looked like the blood had been smoothed out so that her complexion was brown.

Prosecutor: Now, you said that you did notice that she had something in her hair?

Detective Trooper 1: She did.

Prosecutor: Did you ever explore that and find out what that was?

Detective Trooper 1: I did.

Prosecutor: What was that?

Detective Trooper 1: There were two things that I noticed in her hair. I noticed that her hair was wavy and curly: At one time, I asked if she had put product in her hair because I thought it was unusual that her hair almost looked like it was done a while ago, not super fresh, but like her hair was done with product. Women put in spray or gel, it kind of creates a wavy effect, and I asked her about that, I said did you do your hair, is there something in your hair, and she said, no, it's blood. And then I saw something else in that area, and I said, what is this, and it looks to me like a body issue, and I asked what it was from, and she said it was from the dogs. Up at the top of her head, there was a little piece of metal, and it looked like a piece of maybe pop-top metal, but it wasn't, and I asked her about it, and she said that they had a vase that looked like that, so it could be the vase or it could be the lamp, but she did have a vase that looked like that metal.

Prosecutor: So her hair was either curly or frizzy to the point that objects would remain, it wasn't that straight hair?

Detective Trooper 1: It wasn't straight hair. Her hair was curly and wavy, and there were objects in her hair, and there was dried blood in her hair.

Prosecutor: Did she ever discuss her birthdate with you?

Detective Trooper 1: She did. While talking with her and trying to figure out in just casual conversation and trying to figure out her birthday, she said that today was her birthday and that was St. Patrick's Day, March 17th, 2021: She said, "I'm reborn, today is my birthday, I'm reborn today." I don't think I ever got a straight answer out of her for her actual birthday during the conversation.

Prosecutor: But you know that that wasn't her actual birthday?

Detective Trooper 1: That wasn't her actual birthday.

Prosecutor: She said she was reborn?

Detective Trooper 1: She said she was reborn.

Prosecutor: And once you took the samples and you cleaned her up, I guess, for lack of a better term, what happened then? Did you do anything else?

Detective Trooper 1: After the samples were taken and packaged, we transported her to the Manistee County Jail, myself, and Trooper 5.

Prosecutor: And she was, I assume, logged in there: Was there anything of note about that?

Detective Trooper 1: I noticed that she had some other bruises on her arms it almost looked like fingerprint bruises, a couple of them on her forearm, and we stood with her, and she was reluctant to let me leave, she wanted us to stay, and we told her that we couldn't stay with her while she was being booked in. Something that I noted that I had thought was unusual is when as part of the screening process, when an individual is brought into jail, they ask them several questions, and one of the questions that they asked her was if she'd suffered a loss recently, and she said: "yes, it was my mother." She didn't make any reference to Bill.

Prosecutor: You found that to be odd?

Detective Trooper 1: I found that to be – yes, something remarkable at that point.

Prosecutor: Did she ever, at any point in your interview when she was discussing Bill, did she ever discuss their relationship at all?

Detective Trooper 1: She made reference to him being an ex, but no, she didn't talk a lot about him: Even when I found a note, she didn't – she just said no, I don't want to see that right now.

Prosecutor: Okay. So at some point, did she shy away from talking about him?

Detective Trooper 1: It seemed like she was shy about talking about their relationship exactly, but she wasn't exactly shy about when she said that she killed him or the reasons why.

Prosecutor: So it was more the relationship stuff?

Detective Trooper 1: Yes, it was more the relationship stuff.

Prosecutor: And you've referred to, I think Ms. Ross, the person you interviewed: Do you see her in the courtroom today?

Detective Trooper 1: I do.

Prosecutor: Could you please point to her and describe what she's wearing for the record?

Detective Trooper 1: She's wearing an orange jacket around her shoulders and a gray jail suit.

Prosecutor: Your Honor, please let the record reflect this witness has identified the defendant.

Judge: It shall.

MY FATHER'S STORY

Prosecutor: Detective Trooper 1, I've handed you what has been marked People's Proposed Exhibit number 19, do you recognize that?

Detective Trooper 1: I do.

Prosecutor: And can you tell what that is, please?

Detective Trooper 1: It's a picture of Angelee Ross taken at the hospital: I took the photograph before I cleaned her face.

Prosecutor: And so, was that on or about the time she was interviewed?

Detective Trooper 1: Yes, it is.

Prosecutor: And is that a fair and accurate representation of how she looked?

Detective Trooper 1: Yes, it is.

Prosecutor: Your Honor, at this time I would move to admit People's Proposed 19 into evidence.

Judge: People's 19 is received.

Prosecutor: Detective Trooper 1, is there anything unusual about People's 19?

Detective Trooper 1: It struck me as unusual that she was genuinely smiling at me during this photograph, and this is after we'd talked about Bill being dead: I don't see any remorse, reflection, or sadness; I just see someone smiling at me.

Prosecutor: How would you describe, I mean, that smile? Is that the smile of someone who is posing for a picture or something other?

Detective Trooper 1: This looks like the smile of someone posing for a picture, wanting to be cute and pretty.

Prosecutor: Thank you. I don't have any further questions about this witness.

Defense Council: Very briefly. Detective Trooper 1, first, I thank you for your thorough testimony. There was one detail in your report I wanted to ask you about: Do you recall asking her about a scratch on her hand?

Detective Trooper 1: I did recall asking her about a scratch on her hand: I noticed that she had a scratch, I believe it was on her left hand when I was looking at her hands because her right hand was significantly bruised and swollen, but her left hand was less, and I noticed the scratch inside of her left hand.

Defense Council: And what did she tell you?

MY FATHER'S STORY

Detective Trooper 1: She told me that she intentionally cut herself to make sure she was feeling the feelings that she had, to remind herself that she still had faith.

Defense Council: And then she told you, I believe – I need to tell you – and then stopped, and she thanked you for your patience?

Detective Trooper 1: Yes.

Defense Council: And for what you had been doing?

Detective Trooper 1: Yes.

Defense Council: And asked where you'd been all her life?

Detective Trooper 1: Yes.

Defense Council: What did you take that to mean?

Detective Trooper 1: I'm not certain. I didn't understand why she'd said it. She said, "You're so patient, thank you, I'm not worthy. I guess it's just not my, it wasn't my time," is what she said.

Defense Council: You've, as I said, very thoroughly described your interaction and Ms. Ross' responses. As a fellow human being, how did you respond to it? Did you find this person to be completely unusual? Was this a crazy person?

Detective Trooper 1: Well, my interaction with her was something I've not experienced before in my 24-year career. Her mood swings – I've dealt with mood swings with individuals who were under the influence of an intoxicating substance, but she would have these types of swings where she was just super flat and matter-of-fact discussing that she'd killed someone, that she didn't like to do it, but she had to do it because he wasn't chosen, and how he can love, and her swing to being very sexual and enjoying herself, and not having any type of remorse at that time: Other individuals I have interviewed who were suspects in those situations, I've seen remorse: I didn't see that with Angelee that day.

Defense Council: Thank you. No further questions.

Judge: Detective Trooper 1, did she provide any context as to when she cut herself?

Detective Trooper 1: She did not. The only thing I could ascertain was sometime last night, that's the only thing we could figure out was last night.

Judge: Thank you, Detective Trooper 1. You're excused.

Chapter 19: Trooper 5

Prosecutor: Your Honor, I would call Trooper 5 to the stand.

Clerk: Would you please raise your right hand? Do you solemnly swear or affirm that the testimony you give in this case will be the truth, the whole truth, and nothing but the truth, so help you God?

Trooper 5: I do.

Prosecutor: Good Afternoon, Trooper 5. Could you please state and spell your name for the record?

Trooper 5: (REDACTED)

Prosecutor: And sir, what is your occupation, for whom do you work?

Trooper 5: Michigan State Police, currently assigned to the 7th District Headquarters on the fugitive team.

Prosecutor: And on March 17th, 2021, were you a Michigan State Police Trooper?

Trooper 5: I was.

Prosecutor: And on that date, on the morning of that date, did you have contact with someone named Angelee Ross?

Trooper 5: I did.

Prosecutor: And how did that come about? Kindly take me through how that happened, if you would, please.

Trooper 5: During the morning hours, approximately 9:25 in the morning, I was just leaving for this next detail that I'm currently on now, and Detective Trooper 1 was taking over my investigations, so Detective Trooper 1 and I were at the post and then she received a phone call about a homicide that occurred in Manistee County in which that suspect was a female, and Detective Trooper 1 was asked to go to the hospital to be with her for overwatch, and since I was partnered with Detective Trooper 1, I came along with her that day and went to the hospital to meet up with Ms. Ross.

Prosecutor: And what did you find when you got there?

Trooper 5: When we first arrived, Ms. Ross was sitting in the hospital bed in her room. When she was sitting there, she had a hospital gown and some blankets on her legs.

Prosecutor: And what was her demeanor like when you first made contact with her?

Trooper 5: Her demeanor was very calm, seemed kind of spaced out at times, not agitated, not overly worked up, wondering why she was there. I did notice that she did have lots of blood on her face and her hands, and bruising on her arms.

Prosecutor: And at some point, did you speak with her?

Trooper 5: Just briefly. When we first arrived, I activated my patrol in-car recording system, and then when we arrived inside, I realized that Ms. Ross was starting to talk to Detective Trooper 1, and then I activated my recording.

Prosecutor: So Detective Trooper 1 did some interviewing of Ms. Ross: Did you do any of that interviewing, and were you present for that interviewing?

Trooper 5: I more or less listened, and I was present for some of the interviews. When the initial photographs were taken of Ms. Ross, I stepped out for modesty reasons because she was unclothed and wouldn't keep the gown on her, and I wanted to step out for modesty reasons. And so I don't know what was said during that time frame. I was in earshot, the door wasn't completely closed, but I could hear something was going on.

Prosecutor: And at some point, did you come back into the room?

Trooper 5: At some point during the conversation that Detective Trooper 1 was having with Ms. Ross, she came out and said, "Trooper 5, you need to get back in here." She didn't elaborate why or anything like that, but I could tell on her face something was upsetting her, and then I was asked to step back in, and I didn't ask why, and she didn't explain why.

Prosecutor: And when you stepped back in, was Ms. Ross's demeanor different from when you had stepped out?

Trooper 5: It was. When I stepped back in this time, she was more alert, her hospital gown was now off, and her private parts were exposed. She was very in tune with what Detective Trooper 1 had to say. She was making direct eye contact and was very intent with what she had to say. And then I do remember trying to ask Ms. Ross to cover up for modesty reasons, and she said that she was in her natural state and she didn't want to cover up. She wasn't argumentative or anything like that, just a simple statement that this was her natural state and didn't want to be covered up.

Prosecutor: Would you describe her as animated at that point as opposed to before?

Trooper 5: I wouldn't describe her as animated, but if I do, I would describe as whenever Detective Trooper 1 would try to cover up Ms. Ross or position her hair to position her for a photograph or further examination, it was more like a euphoric feeling that Ms. Ross was displaying: She would close her eyes as if she was feeling, I would describe it as a euphoric sensation.

Prosecutor: Are you describing, and I certainly don't want to put words in your mouth, but are you describing sexual overtones or something else?

Trooper 5: That's how I would describe them, yes.

MY FATHER'S STORY

Prosecutor: And did you experience any of that, or was that all directed at Detective Trooper 1?

Trooper 5: I noticed that when I asked the few questions, whether it be trying to convince her to cover up, I did notice she was very in tune with me, but I never – I never put my hands on her to cover up to experience the touching sensation, but I did experience the fact that whenever I would speak she was very, very in tune to what I had to say as well.

Prosecutor: And you were there for the first part of the interview with Detective Trooper 1: Can you kind of tell me what Ms. Ross had indicated about this incident?

Trooper 5: The first part, as in the first initial contact, or before when I got called back into the room?

Prosecutor: The first initial contact.

Trooper 5: So when I first got called in there, I noticed there was blood, blood on her, and when asked what it was from, she said it was from Bill, and in later conversation, she said it was from Bill and the dogs.

Prosecutor: And did she indicate how that had gotten there?

Trooper 5: Ms. Ross stated that it was the blood received from stabbing Bill and the dogs.

Prosecutor: And what was her demeanor when she was discussing those things?

Trooper 5: Still calm. It felt that she was closing her eyes and – I don't want to say envisioning because I don't know what was going on, but it felt like she would close her eyes and kind of think about what she was seeing and then describe it. So when the more direct questions were being asked, I noticed that she would think about what she had to say before she would start describing it, and she made comments that she couldn't believe that was happening, she made comments about energy that she was feeling from there. So the conversations with her were very sporadic and very difficult to follow at times.

Prosecutor: Is that because she was all over the place or?

Trooper 5: All over the place, and then having to be asked the same questions over because of the thought process that was going through, you know, be asked a question and she would say -- like close her eyes and say "I don't understand" or "I'm sorry that I'm blocking you out" and then "can you ask it again" and so those questions, they would get dragged on before you could get a statement.

Prosecutor: And were there any questions or conversations after you had come back into the room?

Trooper 5: There were questions about where the blood came from, asking about how this happened and the bruising that's on the body.

Prosecutor: And what did she say at that time?

Trooper 5: I don't recall. I don't recall what she said about the bruising and how that happened, but I do recall her saying that she had to do it, and she made mention of grabbing a lamp and striking Bill with the lamp, and at one point, she did also say.. and I do apologize, I didn't know this information when it was being presented by Ms. Ross, but she said, "I pointed a gun and it misfired." And then right after that said there was something loud, and then she got scared, and my understanding of where that happened, the lamp and the gun, was upstairs, and my understanding too is then after that, she indicated that he fell down the stairs and then that's when the knife was involved.

Prosecutor: And is that the sum and substance of the conversation after you had returned from the room?

Trooper 5: Sum of the conversation – the sum and substance, yes, that was most of the conversation. A lot, it was too about her talking about the energy that she was receiving from the lights, the energy that she was receiving from the dust particles, and the feeling that was overcoming her and that she had to do this, as in the crime that was committed.

Prosecutor: What did she say about the energy, how did it affect her, how did it make her feel?

Trooper 5: It was telling her what to do.

Prosecutor: Did she indicate if it was a good feeling or a bad feeling or anything like that?

Trooper 5: I don't recall.

Prosecutor: And at some point, Detective Sergeant 1 arrived on scene, correct?

Trooper 5: Correct.

Prosecutor: And he interviewed on his own, correct?

Trooper 5: Correct.

Prosecutor: Were you present for that?

Trooper 5: I was.

Prosecutor: And Detective Trooper 1 was present for that?

Trooper 5: Correct.

Prosecutor: Okay. Thank you. I don't have anything further.

Defense Council: No questions.

Judge: Thank you. You're all set.

Chapter 20: Detective Sergeant 1

Prosecutor: Your Honor, I would call Detective Sergeant 1 to the stand.

Clerk: Please raise your right hand. Do you solemnly swear or affirm that the testimony you give in this case will be the truth, the whole truth, and nothing but the truth, so help you God?

Detective Sergeant 1: I do.

Prosecutor: Good afternoon, Detective Sergeant 1. Could you please state and spell your name for the record?

Detective Sergeant 1: (REDACTED)

Prosecutor: And sir, what is your occupation, for whom do you work?

Detective Sergeant 1: I am a detective sergeant with the Michigan State Police.

Prosecutor: And how long have you been in law enforcement with the Michigan State Police?

Detective Sergeant 1: Twenty-eight years.

Prosecutor: And I want to ask you about the morning of March 17th, 2021, and into the afternoon: Is there something that happened on that day?

Detective Sergeant 1: I was requested – or I was informed of the homicide investigation. At the time, I was out of the count working on a detail, and I was requested to return and assist with that investigation.

Prosecutor: And where was that investigation taking place?

Detective Sergeant 1: Manistee County.

Prosecutor: And what was the role going to be when you returned or came into Manistee County?

Detective Sergeant 1: I was advised a search warrant was being completed for some biological evidence to be taken from the person of Ms. Ross, and I was aware at the time she was at the hospital, and I was asked to serve that search warrant, collect that biological evidence, and attempt an interview with her.

Prosecutor: Okay. And so, at some point, did you make contact with Ms. Ross?

Detective Sergeant 1: I did, it was shortly before 1:00 p.m.

Prosecutor: And when you made contact with her, was she with anybody else at the time?

Detective Sergeant 1: Trooper 5 and Detective Trooper 1 were and had been with her at the hospital.

Prosecutor: And in what room in the hospital did you make contact with her?

Detective Sergeant 1: It was right off the emergency room.

Prosecutor: And what can you tell me about your initial impressions: What did she look like, what was her demeanor like?

Detective Sergeant 1: When I approached her, I introduced myself, and she was unclothed at the time but covered with a blanket, she had not yet been cleaned up by hospital staff to my knowledge, because she still had dried blood on her face and hands.

Prosecutor: How was she behaving at that point?

Detective Sergeant 1: My initial impression and as the interview went on, she appeared extremely out of touch with reality, very calm demeanor, very matter of fact.

Prosecutor: And at some point, you spoke with her about the incident, I'm assuming?

Detective Sergeant 1: Yes.

Prosecutor: And before speaking with her, did you advise her of anything?

Detective Sergeant 1: I was told that she had already been advised of her Miranda rights, but I wished to do it again. And so she was advised of her Miranda rights – Her

Miranda rights once again, and she waived those rights and agreed to speak with me.

Prosecutor: And did you have to read those rights multiple times?

Detective Sergeant 1: Yes.

Prosecutor: And she had previously. You were aware that she had previously been read those by somebody else?

Detective Sergeant 1: Yes, That's correct.

Prosecutor: And eventually, she agreed to speak to you?

Detective Sergeant 1: Yes.

Prosecutor: And she agreed that she understood those rights?

Detective Sergeant 1: Yes.

Prosecutor: So, take me through that: What did she tell you about this?

Detective Sergeant 1: So I initially spoke with her, and much of the interview was also completed by Detective Trooper 1, who was with me. She seemed to have already established a pretty good rapport, so between the two of us, the questions were asked and answered. Initially, I asked her to tell me what happened that morning, and one of the first responses that kind of surprised me were, "You mean the blood bath? The blood bath?" Is what she asked, and so I indicated, yes, that's what I wished to speak about. And she admitted that she had killed Bill, and I asked her to walk me through, and much of what she told me, it was difficult to follow her chronological steps of what happened because there was a lot of what I felt was nonsensical wording that she was providing me for her reasoning. I could only describe she was – believe she was being guided by electricity, static, outside beings, I guess would be the best way to describe what caused her to do this. At no time did she try to evade my questions, and she never tried to minimize what she did. She was very matter-of-fact. It just was given with an explanation that seemed, again, out of touch with reality.

Prosecutor: And did she have a different demeanor with you than she did with Detective Trooper 1?

Detective Sergeant 1: Yes. She, again, wasn't evasive but was somewhat more non-responsive to me and was much more open to speaking with Detective Trooper 1. So, when we would kind of run into where you could see there was. She wasn't answering as freely with me, Detective Trooper 1 would step in and re-ask the question or start asking questions, and she would open up more with her.

Prosecutor: And at some point, did she kind of take you through what happened in this incident?

Detective Sergeant 1: She did.

Prosecutor: What did she say?

Detective Sergeant 1: Again, it's difficult for me to say in exact chronological order because we were kind of jumping around with a lot of stuff that didn't seem to be dealing with reality, but she did admit that she had struck Bill with a lamp and she would give reasons that the lamp had guided her or she was guided to the lamp, somewhat hard to understand. She had, after doing that or at least some point, like I said, chronological is difficult to tell, but she retrieved a firearm, a pistol, and she admitted that it fired off either prematurely or accidentally, and she wasn't able to use that firearm.

Detective Sergeant 1: She then proceeded again with the assault on Bill, and she described it with another lamp hitting him with it. She described retrieving another firearm, another pistol which she had intended to shoot Bill with, but she was unable to cock the weapon and couldn't figure out how to fire it, so she struck Bill with that more than once, she said. Ultimately, she told me that she retrieved a knife, she believes that the knife had at some point been taken upstairs, she described it as a large kitchen knife with a wood handle, and she told me she stabbed Bill and killed him.

Prosecutor: Did she ever describe what happened after he went down the stairs or fell down the stairs?

Detective Sergeant 1: She described him asking at one point, "What are you trying to do, kill me?"

Prosecutor: And did she ever make any statements about, when he fell down the stairs, he didn't die, anything like that you can recall?

Detective Sergeant 1: She did, and I don't remember the exact wording that she used for that; she did tell me that at some point, she knew she had to finish it because he hadn't died.

Prosecutor: And was it your impression in going through this in your testimony here today that there were multiple acts throughout this incident?

Detective Sergeant 1: There was. She had also described how she had killed the dogs, and at some point during the process of this evening, or throughout the evening, she had taken at least one nap either between killing Bill and the dogs or at some point she had taken a nap. So the way it was described to me is it was multiple, multiple assaults on Bill with different items, including at least two lamps, two firearms that she attempted to use, and the kitchen knife.

Prosecutor: Now, she did describe what happened after this, what she did, where she went, those types of things?

Detective Sergeant 1: Following the death of Bill and the dogs, when she decided to leave, she got in her car, and she described that she was being guided, again, it was rather nonsensical, but she was being guided someplace and at some point it was described that she was told to accelerate and that is when she crashed her car. She initially thought that she was being guided to some friend's house, but she didn't know: She was, like I said, being guided by some force, and then she described, yes, that she crashed because she was told to accelerate.

Prosecutor: And Detective Sergeant 1, you've undoubtedly done numerous interviews in your 28 years as a law enforcement officer with the Michigan State Police, correct?

Detective Sergeant 1: Thousands.

Prosecutor: Was this interview bizarre to you?

Detective Sergeant 1: Yes. I'm not a psychiatrist or a psychologist, but I have a pretty good read of people, being that I've interviewed thousands of people, and this would probably be someone who is most out of touch with reality that I've ever spoken with.

Prosecutor: And you say that because of – is it the statements and the demeanor, or what?

Detective Sergeant 1: Both. The demeanor was very nonchalant, very to the point. Many times when I interview somebody that's been involved in a violent incident, they try to minimize their role, evade the police, or don't want to be charged: I did not pick up any of that with her: She was very matter of fact with what she did with her type of reasoning.

Prosecutor: And this interview – when this interview occurred, did you have a recorder going?

Detective Sergeant 1: I did, yes. Just a digital audio recorder was playing.

Prosecutor: And have you listened to that?

Detective Sergeant 1: Yes, I have.

Prosecutor: Okay. And I'm going to show you if I can approach, what's been marked People's Proposed Exhibit number 20: Can you tell me what that is?

Detective Sergeant 1: This is the Michigan State Police incident number for this incident, and it shows that it is the interview with Ms. Ross.

Prosecutor: Your Honor, at this time, I would move to admit People's Proposed 20.

Defense Council: No objection.

Judge: People's Exhibit 20 is received. It can be played.

Prosecutor: Thank you. Your Honor, at this time, I would like to play the video if the court will give me just one second. Your Honor, a dry run was done yesterday, and I think the best way to do this is probably through the TV, so if I could set that up, it would be greatly appreciated.

Prosecutor: Your Honor, I'm prepared to proceed with the interview. I would indicate the disk that I have is almost two hours long. I do not plan on playing the whole thing. Most of it is around the first hour and 10 minutes. I've discussed that with Ms. Defense Council, so I wanted the court to be aware of that. The recorder stayed on for several other things.

Judge: So we have in the bottom right-hand corner I see that there's a time: Tell us what time the audio begins, and then when you shut it off indicate for the record when you're stopping audio.

Prosecutor: Very good, and it looks like it's going to start at 0:00. I will begin that now, and I will indicate when it's done where we stop at.

Clerk: (Audio recording played beginning at 2:26 p.m. and concluded at 3:36 p.m.)

Prosecutor: One hour and 10 minutes, your Honor.

Judge: All right. And just so counsel knows, the court reporter does not transcribe what we just heard: The disk is what is treated as the exhibit.

Prosecutor: Very good. Understood. Thank you. Detective Sergeant 1, there probably isn't much more to say about the interview after that, but just briefly, since that was only audio, what was her body language like during that interview?

Detective Sergeant 1: She was in a reclined position, she was on an examination bed with a blanket covering herself, rather stoic, not a lot of emotion, just very matter of fact and to the point there was never tears or extreme excitement, very relaxed.

Prosecutor: And what was done after the interview?

Detective Sergeant 1: So following that, as I explained earlier, I did have a search warrant to collect biological evidence from her, and she had not been cleaned up as far as I could tell from the hospital, so she had dried blood on her fingers and face, so what I did is just used some sterile cotton tip swabs to collect that dried blood that could be sent to the lab if they needed it for further analysis.

Prosecutor: And did that pretty much wrap up your participation in this investigation?

Detective Sergeant 1: Yes, it did.

Prosecutor: Thank you, sir, I don't have anything further.

Defense Council: No questions, your Honor.

Judge: Thank you, Detective Sergeant 1. You can step down.

Chapter 21: Detective Sergeant 2

Prosecutor: Your Honor, I would call Detective Sergeant 2 to the stand.

Clerk: Would you please raise your right hand? Do you solemnly swear or affirm that the testimony you give in this case will be the truth, the whole truth, and nothing but the truth, so help you God?

Detective Sergeant 2: I do.

Prosecutor: Good Afternoon, Detective Sergeant 2. Could you please state and spell your name for the record?

Detective Sergeant 2: (REDACTED)

Prosecutor: And sir, what is your occupation, for whom do you work?

Detective Sergeant 2: I'm a detective sergeant with the Michigan State Police.

Prosecutor: And how long have you been employed in that capacity?

Detective Sergeant 2: Since 1999.

Prosecutor: And how long have you been with the State Police in total?

MY FATHER'S STORY

Detective Sergeant 2: 1999.

Prosecutor: Okay. Thank you. Now I want to ask you about March 17th, 2021, at approximately 8:00 a.m., is there anything that happened at that time?

Detective Sergeant 2: Yes. So that morning, I was at our office in Manistee monitoring radio traffic and heard Trooper 1 get dispatched to a personal injury crash out in (REDACTED), it escalated a little bit from there to a possible well-being check/homicide, Troopers 2 and 3 were dispatched to that. A short time later, after arriving on the scene, I was contacted by Trooper 3 via radio and advised of his findings.

Prosecutor: And were you at home at the time, or were you at the post?

Detective Sergeant 2: No, I was at our office here in Manistee.

Prosecutor: So, now, once you found out and you were advised by Trooper 3 of what he believed that he had, what did you do, if anything?

Detective Sergeant 2: Yeah, I headed right out to the scene in (REDACTED).

Prosecutor: Now, you headed to that residence: What did you find when you got there?

Detective Sergeant 2: So as soon as I arrived, I made contact with Troopers 2 and 3, there were also two deputies there: The two deputies asked if they were needed any longer, I couldn't think of any reason for them to stick around, so I just had them leave. Trooper 3 then briefed me on what he had, and then we ended up – at that time, he hadn't had any identification on the victim either, so I put on surgical boot coverings, we then went into the residence, one trip in, one trip out, to get a feel for the scene, see what we had, and also an attempt to identify the victim.

Prosecutor: And were you able to identify the deceased individual?

Detective Sergeant 2: Yes. So as soon as we rounded the corner to the left inside the house, his wallet was noticed open. When I entered the house, the whole way in, I took pictures, on the way over, I stopped and took a picture of his driver's license, continued around to where the victim was lying, and was able to confirm that it was being that of Mr. William Johnson.

Prosecutor: So that was Mr. William Johnson's driver's license?

Detective Sergeant 2: It was.

Prosecutor: That was in there, and that was a state of Michigan-issued driver's license?

Detective Sergeant 2: Correct.

Prosecutor: And did that driver's license have the address that matched the address that you were at?

Detective Sergeant 2: It did. He was and is also the only person listed at that address within the secretary of state as well.

Prosecutor: And that photograph on that driver's license matched the person that you had there, the deceased in the residence?

Detective Sergeant 2: Yes.

Prosecutor: And once you had done that, what did you do?

Detective Sergeant 2: So after that, I went upstairs, saw what we had there, walked back out, contacted the lab, and also requested that Trooper 2 start working on search warrants to process the investigation.

Prosecutor: And while you're waiting for those things, that is, for the lab to assemble and the search warrant to get completed, do you just wait outside? How does that work?

Detective Sergeant 2: Yeah. So we try and figure out what we have going on, so kind of get our ducks in a row, so figure out where the suspect was, she was at the hospital, so we arranged for her to be watched over, subsequently arranged for Detective Sergeant 1 to go talk to her and any other tasks that needed to be attended to during that time.

Prosecutor: And do you know how long of a time that was until you were able to enter the residence again?

Detective Sergeant 2: I did not enter the residence until after the lab cleared again. Once I exited that morning, it was not entered again until after the lab was ready to clear the scene. Well, let me take it back. I did talk in there with the medical examiner.

Prosecutor: And was the lab still on scene when the medical examiner arrived?

Detective Sergeant 2: Yes.

Prosecutor: And the medical examiner was who?

Detective Sergeant 2: Medical Examiner 1.

Prosecutor: Now, as you're waiting outside, can you tell me what were the temperatures like that day?

Detective Sergeant 2: It was 33 degrees, there was snow on the ground, and it was fairly chilly.

Prosecutor: And do you know what the temperature was like in the residence?

Detective Sergeant 2: I believe it was 56 degrees, 56 or 58. I took a picture of it, one of those two.

MY FATHER'S STORY

Prosecutor: And once you went back in with the medical examiner, what can you tell me? What happened there?

Detective Sergeant 2: So the lab and the medical examiner kind of discussed what they had found so far, I discussed what I had learned as well. She did an initial check of Mr. Johnson, and then he was subsequently removed and transported to Benzie County for an autopsy.

Prosecutor: And that would be the facility that Medical Examiner 1 would do her autopsies at?

Detective Sergeant 2: Correct.

Prosecutor: And once that happened, did you exit the residence again, or did you go back in, or did you stay in there?

Detective Sergeant 2: Yeah. After the lab left, we did go back in to search for anything else: We also removed the two dogs that were in there at the request of Mr. Johnson's son.

Prosecutor: In your, I guess exploration of the residence, your search of the residence, looking for anything the multiple times that you were in there, at any point did you see any evidence of any illicit drug use?

Detective Sergeant 2: I did not.

Prosecutor: No needles or anything like that, or pipes or anything?

Detective Sergeant 2: No. As a matter of fact, we even requested an MSP K-9 who specializes in narcotics: He searched the residence, and there was nothing found then either.

Prosecutor: As far as the residence itself, obviously you've been in court the whole day, and you've seen some of the people testify: Did it look to you like a struggle had taken place there?

Detective Sergeant 2: Absolutely. You could tell by looking in the closets and in Mr. Johnson's pole barn out there he was very meticulous, he had everything – you could tell he knew where it was, and this looked totally out of character for what was in the house as compared to what may have been in the closet or even his pole barn for that matter.

Prosecutor: And did the house look like it had been meticulously maintained other than something that had happened there?

Detective Sergeant 2: Other than this, yes.

Prosecutor: And so, after the medical examiner had left and after you had gone into the house, just kind of to make sure that nothing was missed and you guys weren't missing anything, what did you do?

Detective Sergeant 2: We secured it the best we could.

Prosecutor: And at some point, did you search the pole barn as well?

Detective Sergeant 2: Yes, yes.

Prosecutor: Was that later on?

Detective Sergeant 2: Well, it was – the lab searched that as well, so when the lab left is when all this took place.

Prosecutor: And was there anything of note about the police barn other than that it was meticulously maintained?

Detective Sergeant 2: Nothing of note, no.

Prosecutor: Now, at some point, did you have contact with Mr. Ross?

Detective Sergeant 2: I did.

Prosecutor: And what can you tell me about that?

Detective Sergeant 2: So this would have been on March 18th, the day after this incident: When I checked my e-mail at that moment, I had received an e-mail from (REDACTED) who was contacted overnight by the jail who said that Ms. Ross had sobered up and wanted to talk to the State Police.

Prosecutor: And so you, I assume, at some point headed to the Manistee County jail to interview her?

Detective Sergeant 2: First thing, yes.

Prosecutor: Where did that interview take place?

Detective Sergeant 2: In the interview room at the Sheriff's office.

Prosecutor: And when you spoke with her, before speaking to her, did you advise her of anything?

Detective Sergeant 2: I did. I advised her of her Miranda warnings.

Prosecutor: And after having heard those, did she indicate to you that she understood those?

Detective Sergeant 2: Yes, she agreed to speak with me.

Prosecutor: What did she tell you about this?

Detective Sergeant 2: Well, at first, I asked her if she knew why I was there, I asked if she knew why she was in jail: She said that she didn't. Then she asked if it had anything to do with William Johnson, and I advised her that it did. So I asked her what she could tell me about it and she said that she murdered him.

Prosecutor: Just like that, 'I murdered him'?

Detective Sergeant 2: Yes.

Prosecutor: What was her demeanor when she said that?

Detective Sergeant 2: She was very, as a matter of fact, wasn't as reserved as what we had heard on the CD: She was pretty forthright, a little more awake, alert, I guess, if you want to call it that.

Prosecutor: And what did she say then? Did you ask her when this happened?

Detective Sergeant 2: Yeah - well, she said that it had happened the day before. So I asked her if she could tell me a little bit more about it. She had stated that - during the interview, she had stated that there was a purge that was happening, the states were conducting a purge and mass genocide: She also stated that she used the knife to murder Mr. Johnson. During the interview also, there were points in it where she thought that they were removing her memory, or she had mentioned at one time that I was removing her memory. I told her I didn't have the power to remove her memory. She stated okay and that was kind of fine with that answer, which was a little odd.

Prosecutor: And when she said that she had murdered him and that was yesterday, did she say where it had taken place?

Detective Sergeant 2: At his house.

Prosecutor: And once she was okay with you indicating to her that you didn't have the power to remove her memory, did she say anything else?

Detective Sergeant 2: She talked a little bit more. We discussed what she had done that day. I asked her about her contact with the State Trooper, it would have been two days prior, so the evening of the 16th, she talked about that a little bit, how she took her son back to Cadillac, she then went to Walmart, purchased two sleeping bags, a fleece blanket and something else, I don't recall what the other thing is offhand, and then proceeded back to Mr. Johnson's residence.

Prosecutor: And was she able at that point to relate kind of the events of that night, or at least how the evening began?

Detective Sergeant 2: Yes, so she said that when she was there Mr. Johnson wasn't home from work yet. She - as soon as he got home, he had made dinner; she didn't eat because she was extremely scared, I think it was what she had said, because of the purge that was coming. She said that she had told Bill about it, but he didn't believe her. I asked her what she thought about him not believing her, and she didn't answer. She said. I asked her if there was an argument: There didn't appear to be an argument. I asked if there was just talking: She said there was not much talking.

Prosecutor: Did you ever ask her what there was if there wasn't much talking?

MY FATHER'S STORY

Detective Sergeant 2: She just said again that she murdered him.

Prosecutor: And did she ever say when what time it happened?

Detective Sergeant 2: She said it was dark. There were no specific times given for anything. We kind of just went off daylight or darkness.

Prosecutor: And Detective Sergeant 2, was this a normal interview?

Detective Sergeant 2: I wouldn't say a normal interview, no. You know, during the interview, she would stop and kind of look to one side, and, you know, say that they were currently taking her memories from her whenever she was being asked something, you know, so she did that twice.

Prosecutor: Was she relaying back and forth about memories being gone and then maybe coming back?

Detective Sergeant 2: She said that she could remember part, but then she'd remember parts of it, and then they'd be gone.

Prosecutor: Well, did she ever mention anything about the dogs?

Detective Sergeant 2: She did. I asked her what she did after she had killed William. She stated that she took the knife and stabbed the dogs. She said that the big dog, Zena, was Bill's, the other dog was a lady named (REDACTED) dog. She also stated that she had sex with (REDACTED'S) dog.

Prosecutor: And when she had said that that dog belonged to (REDACTED), did you ask her who (REDACTED) was?

Detective Sergeant 2: Yeah. She stated it was somebody who needed to be put down.

Prosecutor: What did you take that to mean?

Detective Sergeant 2: Well, I didn't quite understand it. She worked with her at (REDACTED) at some point. She had said that she tried helping her, she possibly had schizophrenia, she had taken her to the hospital, and Ms. Ross had ended up with (REDACTED)'s stuff.

Prosecutor: Now, did she talk about her background at an, where she had been employed, any of those types of things?

Detective Sergeant 2: She did. She stated that she moved up here I believe it was 2018, and she was living in the Metro Detroit area. She said that she had worked at (REDACTED). She moved up here, moved in with Bill, lived with him for I think it was a year and a half, she moved out, lived in a shelter for a short time, and then she ended up moving to I think it was (REDACTED) in Cadillac.

Prosecutor: And did the conversation ever turn back to the events of the evening/early morning hours on the 17th?

Detective Sergeant 2: I did ask her about what happened afterwards: She stated that she had left the house and drove to Manistee, ended up getting in a traffic crash, she didn't know where it was or who they were, she didn't know if they were injured.

Judge: She stated she had traveled to Manistee.

Detective Sergeant 2: Yes.

Prosecutor: And did you ever explore that with her?

Detective Sergeant 2: No. Towards the end of the interview, you could tell she was appearing to be very stressed out, just breathing real heavy, and it just seemed like it wasn't going to be going anywhere else without further antagonizing her, I guess if you want to put it that way. She just seemed very stressed out at the end.

Prosecutor: And it was your impression that she had initially requested to speak to somebody from the police department?

Detective Sergeant 2: Yes, that's what I was told, yes.

Prosecutor: But when you got there, she didn't know – she indicated she didn't know why you were there?

Detective Sergeant 2: Correct.

Prosecutor: You've already touched upon it some, Detective Sergeant 2, but could you touch upon it a little bit about her body language and her demeanor change?

Detective Sergeant 2: No, no. The only time it did change is if she looked up to the left or the right, I don't recall which it was offhand, but when her memories were being taken from her. Other than that it was pretty much, you know, at the time we had masks on so we couldn't, you know, the COVID masks, so we couldn't see any facial expressions, but I mean, you could see eyeballs, so that was the only thing I could notice.

Prosecutor: And you have - you've indicated that the interview was with Ms. Ross: do you see her here in the courtroom today?

Detective Sergeant 2: Yes, at the defendant's table wearing the orange jacket.

Prosecutor: Please let the record reflect the witness identified as the defendant.

Judge: It shall. Was the interview videotaped?

Detective Sergeant 2: It was.

Prosecutor: Thank you. I don't have anything further at this time.

Defense Council: Thank you. Detective Sergeant 2, I apologize in advance if my questions seem disjointed or disconnected from what you've been discussing, but as part of your – you were the chief investigating officer in this case, correct?

Detective Sergeant 2: Right.

Defense Council: And as part of your investigation, did you review a urine drug screen that was conducted on 3-18 for Angelee Ross?

Detective Sergeant 2: Yes, I did.

Defense Council: And I'm going to approach, and it's been marked as Defendant's Exhibit A: Is that the document that you reviewed?

Detective Sergeant 2: It is.

Defense Council: And it's true, is it not, that urine drug screen indicates that methamphetamine was not detected, correct?

Detective Sergeant 2: Correct.

Defense Council: Thank you. And Amphetamine was, correct?

Detective Sergeant 2: Correct.

Judge: Do we agree, Mr. Prosecutor, that Adderall is a form of Amphetamine?

Prosecutor: Adderall is Amphetamine, Your Honor.

Defense Council: I'm offering Defendant's Exhibit A into evidence.

Judge: Defendant's Exhibit A is received.

Defense Council: Detective Sergeant 2, also as part of your investigation you retrieved some jail logs, is that correct?

Detective Sergeant 2: That is correct.

Defense Council: I'm going to show you what's been marked as Defendant's D and ask you to take a look at it and tell me if you can identify that for me.

Detective Sergeant 2: That was the jail log that you had requested.

Defense Council: And it's dated?

Detective Sergeant 2: 3-29 of '21.

Defense Council: And there's an entry on there relative to Angelee Ross specifically, correct?

Detective Sergeant 2: Yes, there is, at 8:22 a.m.

Defense Council: And what does it say?

Detective Sergeant 2: "Ross spreads feces in the cell, on the door, windows, and phone."

Defense Council: I would offer Defendant's Exhibit B as evidence at this time.

Judge: Defendant's Exhibit B is received.

Defense Council: And finally, Detective Sergeant, you, as part of your investigation, retrieved several 911 calls from Manistee County Sheriff's Department, is that correct?

Detective Sergeant 2: That is correct.

Defense Council: Including a call that Ms. Ross made the night before this incident occurred, correct?

Detective Sergeant 2: Correct.

Defense Council: Your Honor, I would ask to play defendant's Exhibit C, It's approximately seven minutes long, I believe.

Judge: Defendant's Exhibit C is received into evidence, and yes, you may.

Clerk: (Audio recording played beginning at 4:08 p.m. and ended at 4:18 p.m.)

Defense Council: Your Honor, the start time was 0:00, stop time was 25:06 on Exhibit C.

Judge: We didn't listen to 25 minutes' worth of the exhibit.

Prosecutor: We did not, your Honor. My understanding is that was the call from March 15th.

Defense Council: Yes.

Prosecutor: There may be another call on here that is not being played.

Judge: That would have been before this one?

Prosecutor: There's one from the 16th as well.

Judge: So it was eight minutes and 41 seconds long?

Defense Council: Yes, Your Honor.

Judge: That will be what is reflected in evidence as Defendant's Exhibit C is only that portion of – it appeared it was on a thumb drive.

Defense Council: Yes. Thank you, Your Honor. Detective Sergeant 2, did you listen to the remainder of the recording on that thumb drive?

Detective Sergeant 2: I did. It was a phone call from Deputy (REDACTED) to dispatch advising how he handled the incident.

Defense Council: And how did he handle the incident?

Detective Sergeant 2: He did not respond to the location. He made a phone call, he spoke with both Ms. Ross and Mr. Johnson: He said Mr. Johnson appeared perfectly normal and Mr. Johnson advised him that all of his guns were locked and secured, he was going to try and get Ms. Ross in for an evaluation at some point. Deputy (REDACTED) also said that they might end up back out there for involuntary transport.

Defense Council: And in fact, he described Ms. Ross as being nuts, correct?

Detective Sergeant 2: He did.

Defense Council: Thank you very much. Nothing further.

Judge: All right. Thank you, Detective Sergeant, 2. You may step down. Do you have any other witnesses today, Mr. Prosecutor?

Prosecutor: Your Honor, not today. I do have Medical Examiner 1 and Funeral Home Director subpoenaed for tomorrow morning. I do not have any other witnesses.

Judge: After Medical Examiner 1 and Funeral Home Director testify, do you have any additional witnesses?

Prosecutor: I do not.

Judge: And you have several, is that correct?

Defense Council: I do. The forensic Psychologist and the independent expert.

Judge: You are going to call the doctors?

Defense Council: I'm going to call both doctors, they will be appearing by Zoom, your Honor.

Judge: What time are you available?

Defense Council: They are available whenever I call them: They've made themselves available all day.

Judge: And you would like the court to hear from the doctors last?

Defense Council: Yes.

Judge: All right. Then if there's nothing further, we will be in recess for the day.

Clerk: All rise!

Chapter 22: The Aftermath of Day 1

As the first day of the hearing came to a close, we all filed out into the hallway, letting out big sighs. The Prosecutor, Detective Sergeant, and Detective Sergeant 2 followed us, and we started chatting. The Prosecutor kicked off the conversation by asking for our thoughts on how his strategy was going. We all praised him for doing a fantastic job in laying out the story and presenting all the details. Then, he mentioned, "Today was tough, but tomorrow is going to be even harder in court."

His statement had us in awe. We couldn't believe that the second day would be more challenging than the first.

After leaving the courthouse, we headed back to the hotel and decided to take an hour to rest and unwind before dinner. I collapsed onto the bed, trying to process all the information I had heard in court. Even as a horror movie lover, I couldn't even fathom some of the things that were described.

Eventually, we made our way to the restaurant for dinner. It was wonderful to have all these people from different parts of my father's and my life gathered at one table, but there was an odd tension in the air. Our conversations would start on one topic but circle back to something that was said in court. We discussed every aspect related to the case, occasionally shifting to other subjects like life, family, and food, only to be pulled back into the courtroom discussions. It was difficult for all of us to process the disturbing things that had been revealed.

Finally, we finished up our dinner, and all agreed that it was time to head back to the hotel. My two friends and I decided to head to my room. We popped open a bottle of wine and started talking about all the testimonies we had heard throughout the day. Eventually, I had to kick my friends out because all I wanted was a hot shower and a good night's sleep. Even though I couldn't shake this restless feeling, exhaustion took over as soon as I hit the bed after showering, and I passed out right away.

The next morning, my alarm blared. I reached over and silenced it, but that sinking feeling in my stomach was already there. After a few minutes of mustering up the willpower, I dragged myself out of bed and started getting ready for the day.

With my cold brew coffee in hand, I shuffled out of my room and made my way down to the hotel's sitting area where breakfast was served. As I entered the room, I found everyone already seated, patiently waiting for me. I greeted them all with a smile, but my attention was drawn to a man sitting alone in the background. I recognized him from the courtroom gallery yesterday.

Joining the group, I enjoyed my cold brew coffee. Eventually, I headed back to my room to grab my sweater.

MY FATHER'S STORY

When I got back, I saw my mom chatting with this guy. She spotted me and motioned for me to join them. I walked over, and my mom said, "Hey, Eric, this man wants to talk to you."

I replied, "Sure, what's up?"

The guy seemed really nervous. Goosebumps covered his arms, and he had this lost expression on his face.

He said, "Um...I'm Angelee's stepbrother...I'm so sorry." Then, out of nowhere, he pulled me into a tight bear hug.

After letting go, he said, "I only met your dad a few times, but he was an amazing man." He added, "If you ever need anything, don't hesitate to reach out to me." Shocked, all I could say back was, "Thank you. I appreciate it."

Soon, we wrapped up the conversation and regrouped in the hotel lobby. We all hopped into our cars and drove to the courthouse.

Once we arrived, we parked and made our way across the parking lot toward the entrance. The same court officer from yesterday greeted us with a friendlier tone, maybe because he realized we weren't troublemakers despite the circumstances. As we passed through the metal detector, he asked if we had brought extra tissues because it was going to be a tough day in court. As if my stomach wasn't already uneasy enough, it somehow managed to feel even worse.

We made our way up to the third-floor courtroom, found our seats, and settled in, just like the day before. The Prosecutor, Detective Sergeant, and Detective Sergeant 2 entered the room and greeted us. We huddled around the prosecutor's table and discussed the game plan for the day. After wrapping up our discussion, we returned to our seats. That's when the Defense Council walked in. She glanced at all of us and gave a friendly greeting before placing her belongings on the defense table.

She took out a box of Kleenex and approached me. Placing the Kleenex on the railing that separated the gallery from the rest of the court, she said, "I'm truly sorry, but today is going to be an incredibly hard day."

Just moments later, we heard the familiar voice of the court clerk announcing, "All rise! People versus Angelee Ross, File number 21-5181-FC."

Chapter 23: Funeral Home Director

Judge: Good Morning, Mr. Prosecutor. Do you have another witness?

Prosecutor: Good Morning, Your Honor. On behalf of the People, I do, Your Honor. I would begin this morning with Mr. Funeral Home Director.

Clerk: Would you please raise your right hand? Do you solemnly swear or affirm that any testimony you give in this case will be the truth, the whole truth, and nothing but the truth, so help you God?

Funeral Home Director: I do.

Prosecutor: Good morning, Mr. Funeral Home Director. Could you state and spell your name for the record?

Funeral Home Director: (REDACTED)

Prosecutor: Thank you. And sir, what is your occupation, for whom do you work?

Funeral Home Director: I own the funeral home, and we also provide transport service for the Benzie and Manistee counties' medical examiner's office.

Prosecutor: And so you work with Medical Examiner 1?

Funeral Home Director: This is correct.

Prosecutor: And where were you on the afternoon of March 17th, 2021?

Funeral Home Director: I was with Medical Examiner 1 on the death call for Mr. Johnson.

Prosecutor: And what can you tell me about that?

Funeral Home Director: We provided transport from the scene to Paul Oliver Hospital in Frankfort for X-rays and then transported to the funeral home.

Prosecutor: And were you responsible for that transportation?

Funeral Home Director: Yes, I was.

Prosecutor: And when you got to the scene, where was the scene, by the way?

Funeral Home Director: The scene was home in (REDACTED). Mr. Johnson was at the bottom of the stairs.

Prosecutor: And is there a procedure that you go through when you're transporting a body?

Funeral Home Director: Yes, so from the scene, what we do is he's placed in a body transport pouch: once they're placed in a transport pouch, a seal is affixed to that so the body transportation pouch cannot be opened, and that's not opened until the time of autopsy.

Prosecutor: And when you take an individual from a scene, does it go to - the individual go to the funeral home?

Funeral Home Director: Well, in this circumstance, we took him to Paul Oliver for X-rays, so the body pouch was not opened, so everything remained sealed, again, because that way it doesn't contaminate any of the evidence. Then we transported him to the funeral home where he was placed in refrigeration for autopsy with Medical Examiner 1.

Prosecutor: And at the funeral home, is that secured storage as well?

Funeral Home Director: Yes. As a matter of fact. It's secured and also videoed.

Prosecutor: And does that, when a body is placed there, is that body not disturbed again until Medical Examiner 1 is involved?

Funeral Home Director: That is correct. Medical Examiner 1 will come to the funeral home, and when she arrives, the body is placed in the area for autopsy. The seal is not cut until Medical Examiner 1 is in the room.

Prosecutor: And is that generally done, that seal being cut, is that done in your presence?

Funeral Home Director: Yes, and I usually do that.

Prosecutor: And did you do that in this case?

Funeral Home Director: Yes, I did.

Prosecutor: And when you went to cut that seal, was that in the same condition as it previously was when you had affixed that?

Funeral Home Director: Oh, yes, it's a sealed bag.

Prosecutor: And that would indicate that nothing had been contaminated?

Funeral Home Director: Nothing has been contaminated.

Prosecutor: And did you assist Medical Examiner 1 in any other way on this case?

Funeral Home Director: Yes, I assisted her with the autopsy.

Prosecutor: And is that a usual role for you that you would assist in the autopsy?

Funeral Home Director: With my background, I assist Medical Examiner 1 with those.

Prosecutor: But Medical Examiner 1 runs the main autopsy? So you just help her?

Funeral Home Director: I assist her, correct.

MY FATHER'S STORY

Prosecutor: Very good. Thank you, Mr. Funeral Home Director. I don't have anything further at this time.

Defense Council: No questions, Your Honor.

Judge: Thank you, Mr. Funeral Home Director.

Chapter 24: Medical Examiner 1

Prosecutor: Your Honor, I would call Medical Examiner 1 to the stand.

Clerk: Would you please raise your right hand? Do you solemnly swear or affirm that any testimony you give in this case will be the truth, the whole truth, and nothing but the truth, so help you God?

Medical Examiner 1: Yes, I do.

Judge: Right next to me, Medical Examiner 1, please. Good Morning.

Prosecutor: Good morning, Medical Examiner 1. Could you please state and spell your name for the record?

Medical Examiner 1: My name is (REDACTED).

Prosecutor: Doctor, what is your occupation, and for whom do you work?

Medical Examiner 1: My job title right now is the regional medical examiner for the counties of Manistee and Benzie.

Prosecutor: And are you a licensed physician in the state of Michigan?

Medical Examiner 1: Yes, I am.

Prosecutor: And where did you go to medical school?

Medical Examiner 1: At (REDACTED), College of osteopathic medicine.

Prosecutor: And where did you do your residency?

Medical Examiner 1: At (REDACTED).

Prosecutor: And how long have you been employed as a medical examiner for Manistee and Benzie counties?

Medical Examiner 1: It's been about six years now.

Prosecutor: Have you worked as a medical examiner or in that capacity anywhere else?

Medical Examiner 1: Yes, I did.

Prosecutor: And where have you worked, and for how long?

Medical Examiner 1: I was a deputy medical examiner for the District of Columbia in Washington, D.C., for 12 years.

Prosecutor: And throughout your career, how many autopsies do you think that you've performed?

Medical Examiner 1: About 4,000.

Prosecutor: And have you testified before? How many times do you think you've testified before?

Medical Examiner 1: When I worked in D.C., I testified about 10 to 12 times a year, so it's close to 100 times.

Prosecutor: And have you been qualified as an expert before?

Medical Examiner 1: Yes I have.

Prosecutor: In what field?

Medical Examiner 1: Forensic Pathology.

Prosecutor: And by what courts, if you can recall?

Medical Examiner 1: The first time I testified was in Baltimore City and Baltimore County, that was during my fellowship in Baltimore. My first job was as a contract medical examiner in Oakland County, Michigan, and I did testify in Jackson, Michigan, at a homicide trial there, and the rest of the times that I've testified mostly have been back east in D.C. courts, in Maryland, in West Virginia, and also in Virginia.

Prosecutor: And you have previously testified in Manistee County, have you not?

Medical Examiner 1: I believe I have, yes.

Prosecutor: And in the courts that you've testified, you've been qualified as an expert in forensic pathology previously?

Medical Examiner 1: Yes.

Prosecutor: Your Honor, at this time, I would move to have Medical Examiner 1 recognized as an expert in the field of forensic pathology.

Judge: Medical Examiner 1 will be received as an expert in the field of forensic pathology and allowed to testify in opinion form according to our Rules of Evidence.

Prosecutor: Medical Examiner 1, I'm going to ask you about March 17th, 2021: Did you respond to an address in (REDACTED) and make contact with Mr. William Johnson?

Medical Examiner 1: Yes, I did.

Prosecutor: And what can you tell me about that?

Medical Examiner 1: I was notified that there was a case, a death that had occurred that required an investigation, and I have a contract with Mr. Funeral Home Director for transports: I met him at the funeral home, and in an appropriate vehicle with the appropriate equipment we went to the scene together. And when I arrived there, State Police troopers met us and took us into Mr. Johnson's home.

Prosecutor: And as a medical examiner, when you're arriving on scene and potentially examining a body, are there certain things that you look for?

Medical Examiner 1: Well, the first thing I do is make sure that there is a law enforcement Officer with me at all times, and like I say, they walked me through the scene. I asked to see Mr. Johnson, of course, first, and then there were other places in the home where the evidence technicians and the law enforcement officers on the scene felt that there were things that I needed to see because they were potentially used as weapons.

Prosecutor: And were you able to learn anything from either view of the scene or view of how Mr. Johnson was placed or how his body was positioned or the type of wounds that were apparent to you right then and there?

Medical Examiner 1: He did appear to have blunt-force trauma and sharp-force wounds. The officers on the scene pointed out to me that there was a shell casing on the floor, I believe in an upstairs loft area, and so they were concerned that Mr. Johnson may also have a gunshot wound; for that reason, when I left the scene that day, we did not go directly back to where the autopsy was going to take place; we made phone calls and called the radiology department at Paul Oliver Hospital and asked if they would perform X-rays for us.

Prosecutor: And you, in fact, had those x-rays done and you considered those part of your examination and autopsy of Mr. Johnson?

Medical Examiner 1: Those were done on the same day that we went to the scene, those were done on March 17th; my examination – the autopsy took place on March 18th.

Prosecutor: Were you privy to the results of the x-rays on March 17th? Were the immediate?

Medical Examiner 1: Yes.

Prosecutor: And was there – did you find anything as a result of those x-rays?

Medical Examiner 1: We do not see anything that looked like a projectile, a ballistic projectile, or bullet fragments, and I hadn't noticed anything that I could tell for sure, you know, was a gunshot wound at the scene, so at that point, I started to think maybe he didn't have any ballistic wounds.

Prosecutor: And you previously indicated that the autopsy was done on March 18th?

Medical Examiner 1: Yes.

Prosecutor: And that was done where?

Medical Examiner 1: At (REDACTED).

Prosecutor: And you have a facility there specifically set up to conduct these types of autopsies?

Medical Examiner 1: It's used also by the funeral director, but yes, we have added things to that facility so that I can do my exams.

Prosecutor: Yeah. I guess my question went to, is it appropriate, and do you have everything you need there to conduct a proper autopsy?

Medical Examiner 1: Yes.

Prosecutor: And so what time of the day did you begin your autopsy, Doctor?

Medical Examiner 1: It was about 10:00 a.m. I believe.

Prosecutor: And when you complete an autopsy, do you do what would be considered an autopsy report? And did you do that with Mr. Johnson's case?

Medical Examiner 1: Yes, I did.

Prosecutor: Is that autopsy report, do you keep that in the ordinary course of business?

Medical Examiner 1: Yes.

Prosecutor: Doctor, I've handed you what has previously been marked as People's Proposed Exhibit number 21, do you recognize that?

Medical Examiner 1: This is the text of the report that I prepared and also a copy of the toxicology results.

Prosecutor: And is that a complete copy of your text and toxicology results?

MY FATHER'S STORY

Medical Examiner 1: Yes.

Prosecutor: Your Honor, at this time I would move to admit People's Proposed Exhibit number 21 into evidence.

Judge: Peoples Exhibit 21 is received.

Prosecutor: Doctor, what can you tell me about the autopsy itself?

Medical Examiner 1: We went very slowly, we took our time because sharp-force wounds are what usually involves the person and their assailant being close together, and so there's usually a lot of evidence collection that is requested, and we were very careful to examine Mr. Johnson's clothing and the surfaces of his body to collect trace evidence if it was there.

Prosecutor: And when you conduct an autopsy, do you start at one area of the body and work your way to another? How does that work? Just kind of take me through how you normally do things.

Medical Examiner 1: There is a standard protocol for forensic autopsies, and with a case involving injuries, the first concern is always collecting that evidence. You cannot do any washing or rinsing, or, you know, taking clothes off or anything until that evidence collection is done. And then, you know, one by one body is undressed, and lots of photographs are taken right from the beginning. Every time we find something we consider to be of evidentiary value, it is photographed in place, and then it's collected and appropriately packaged. Some things were requested in terms of swabs, so we did that, and those are appropriately dried and then packaged, and then when you get to the appropriate time... you know, I'm trying to document everything as we go along, at the appropriate time you do wash the body and this is the only way to observe what is injury and what is dried blood.

Prosecutor: And you indicated that you collect evidence: You would collect things such as clothing potentially to preserve the evidentiary value, and you would turn those things over to law enforcement?

Medical Examiner 1: Yes.

Prosecutor: Do you ever, as part of your analysis, examine the clothing to determine if the clothing would give you any kind of indication of what type of injuries the victim may have sustained?

Medical Examiner: Well, we did that in this case. There were slit-like defects in Mr. Johnson's shirt over his chest and abdomen that were correspondent to where he had injuries on his chest and abdomen, and so, yeah, we noticed that, and we don't have to usually suggest that the police take things, they know that evidence has value and they, you know, they were willing to collect everything that we observed.

Prosecutor: And there were officers present during the autopsy?

Medical Examiner 1: Yes, continuously.

Prosecutor: Once you got to the point where you could wash the body and clean it so that you could determine where the wounds potentially may be, what did you do next?

Medical Examiner 1: I measured the wounds and, again, that took a little time. But Mr. Johnson had, as I said before, blunt-force trauma, he had sharp-force wounds, both cutting wounds and stab wounds, and I document where those are on the body, measuring the distance from the top of the head to the, you know, to the wound for the sharp-force wounds, and for the blunt-force trauma if there's a laceration or contusion I measure those as well.

Prosecutor: And at some point, you open up the body correct?

Medical Examiner 1: Yes.

Prosecutor: And do you start at a certain point on the body and work your way to an endpoint?

Medical Examiner 1: Yes. Again, there's a standard protocol for doing a forensic autopsy. Once we're at the point where we can make a V incision and open the body cavities, in this case, we also were following wound tracts into the chest cavities and the abdomen, and so, again, that slows you down, but that's the... really the only way that you're going to observe the tracts of the stab wounds and get an idea of their depth and what is injured along the tract.

Prosecutor: Now, in your report, you document the evidence of injuries, and it almost appears that you begin with the head and neck area, at least in your report: is that how... is that the order when you are doing the examination?

Medical Examiner 1: It... No, it's not. Documenting, yes, I start from the head and work my way down, but the autopsy protocol requires that the body cavities are opened once you get to that part of the examination, and then the head and skull and brain are examined, and the last part of the autopsy procedure would be the dissection of the neck.

Prosecutor: Doctor, if you could take me through your findings of injuries to Mr. Johnson, starting with the way they're laid out in your report, and I think that would start with the head area and the scalp, if you could kind of take me through your findings and explain to me what you found that would be helpful. I would appreciate that if you could start with the scalp.

Medical Examiner 1: First of all, in the section of the report that pertains to the injuries, I do have a disclaimer statement that I'm starting with the wounds to the head and working my way down totally just for the organization of the report. The fact is, I don't know which of these injuries occurred first. You know, there are some characteristics of a wound that will tell you how vital a person was when they received that injury, and for others, they look like they could almost be post-mortem, and I do mention that as I describe the wounds, but the real truth is I don't know the order of the wounds in actuality, but I'm describing them in this order because, as you say, I'm working from the top of the head down to the feet.

Prosecutor: So if you could begin with, obviously, the top of the head and the scalp.

Medical Examiner 1: So I start with the injuries to the scalp, and we found nine lacerations of the scalp and seven abrasions, and there were different characteristics of some of these wounds: some of them were angular shaped, what I could describe as a pattern wound because they help you to identify what type of instrument was used to create that wound.

Prosecutor: And so, with an angular-shaped wound, what would that tell you?

Medical Examiner 1: Well, for instance, Mr. Johnson had some wounds that had like an L-shape on his scalp, some lacerations: There were a few of them that intersected, and that would kind of make us look for something that had that shape, a blunt object that had something with a 90-degree angle.

Prosecutor: With a square or rectangular bottom potentially?

Medical Examiner 1: Yeah.

Prosecutor: And you talk too about lacerations: is a laceration always a cut or could it be from a split from force?

Medical Examiner 1: A laceration is a split from a forceful below. It does not involve a sharp implement at all. Lacerations have, as one of their identifying characteristics, what we call tissue bridges, and that are usually little blood vessels that haven't broken, and the other tissues around those blood vessels have separated, and if you look at a wound that is a tear in the skin and you see little soft tissue bridges across that wound, then that was caused by a blunt object striking right in that area, that tears in the skin were caused by a blunt impact rather than a sharp instrument.

Prosecutor: And as far as the abrasions, can you explain, I guess, what an abrasion is in medical terms?

Medical Examiner 1: Abrasion is just a scrape, kind of by friction. There's a sloughing offof the epidermis, sometimes they go a little deeper, sometimes they are associated with a contusion as well, and sometimes that contused tissue can be edematous either because of fluid collecting in the tissue or blood collecting in that tissue, but those would all be examples of tissue wounds that are considered blunt trauma.

Prosecutor: What did you find next?

Judge: I have one question, Mr. Prosecutor. Doctor, if I add the number of lacerations to the abrasions, I arrive at 16: Does that have any significance in the number of times that Mr. Johnson may have been struck in that area? Can I reach any conclusions in that way?

Medical Examiner 1: I say several areas where I can see injury has occurred because, at the end of that, you can add those up, and that would be the minimum number of impacts to his scalp.

Judge: Thank you.

Medical Examiner 1: It's... you know, people may be struck more than once in the same place, but there's a minimum Of 16 impacts to the scalp.

Prosecutor: What did you find next, Doctor?

Medical Examiner 1: The next area where I describe soft tissue and also some underlying fractures in the face. Mr. Johnson had eight lacerations of his facial soft tissue, and there were six abraded areas, and I describe those: Again, they have certain geometrical shapes that might help us identify what caused those wounds. In particular, there's an area of laceration at the outer comer of Mr. Johnson's right eve, and there was an underlying fracture of the orbital rim underneath there. We collected a tiny piece of some synthetic tissue from inside that wound, and that was submitted as evidence. In the x-rays and also when it was time to examine Mr. Johnson's brain and base of the skull, I noted that not only was there a fracture of the orbital rim, but there were also fractures of the right orbital roof which is a thin bone forming the top of the orbital cavity, and there were also like some diastatic fractures of the basilar skull.

Prosecutor: And these fractures that you speak of, is there any way to tell or differentiate whether these fractures occurred due to a fall or due to a strike?

Medical Examiner 1: All I can say is that there was an impact there that was strong enough to cause the bone to fracture and the tissue to split.

Prosecutor: So, a significant impact?

Medical Examiner 1: Yes.

Prosecutor: Please continue, Doctor, with the next findings.

Medical Examiner 1: The next place of injury that I describe is, some injuries were his ear and to the temple area and the sides of his mouth, and some of them were not actually on his face or his scalp, so when I describe the injuries to the ear I decided to describe that separately. One thing I also didn't mention when we were talking about facial injuries, there were additional fractures of Mr. Johnson's facial bones: He had a fracture of the left nasal bone and his nasal cartilage was dislocated towards the left. He also had fractures of the upper dental arch and also the mandible, and there were no, like, 10 displacements of the teeth or anything, and the fracture of the upper dental arch was not displaced at all; one of the mandibles was slightly displaced.

Prosecutor: And is there any way you'd be able to differentiate if this was an old fracture that was re-healed as opposed to a more recent one?

Medical Examiner 1: The injuries that I'm describing here show no signs of healing.

Prosecutor: And that would tell you what?

Medical Examiner 1: That they occurred on the day of his death. The only thing that, where I did describe that I didn't know whether it was due to what he went through before his death or previous in his life was he had a chipped tooth: The lateral incisor on one of his teeth was chipped, and the area where the tooth was chipped it was sharp, but still, I can't say whether or not somebody could have a picture of him three years ago with that chipped tooth, so I mentioned it, but I don't know that it is part of this episode.

Medical Examiner 1: The next thing that I described is some cutting wounds on the front of his neck, and I believe he had one other cutting wound on the left side of his neck: These were not very deep, about an eighth of an inch at the most, and one of these two cutting wounds across the front of his neck did make a mark on his thyroid cartilage which is what forms Adam's apple: other than that, there weren't injuries due to those cutting wounds that injured like major blood vessels or anything like that, they were just soft tissue. The next thing that I describe are abrasions of his right shoulder, the back of his neck, and also the right scapular region and the center of his back: these were abrasions, but they were large, and I... I described them because there was a pattern that you could recognize on the... I believe on the right side of his back on the scapular region, the pattern of that wound matched the fabric pattern of the shirt, the inside of the shirt that Mr. Johnson was wearing.

Prosecutor: Would that indicate anything to you?

Medical Examiner 1: Well, it indicates that he, you know, he was laying on the shirt, but I had seen before where this very same type of injury occurred in someone who was dragged.

Prosecutor: If you would continue, Doctor, to your next findings.

Medical Examiner 1: The next area I describe soft tissue wounds are abrasions of his forearms and hands. Mr. Johnson had some cutting wounds on his fingers, and he had some abrasions on the back of his hands and his forearms, just bruising, you know, areas of bruising and injuries to the hands and forearms: some people call those defensive wounds.

Prosecutor: Doctor, have you seen those wounds on hands and forearms and fingers before?

Medical Examiner 1: Yes.

Prosecutor: And in your experience, have those previously been characterized as defensive wounds?

Medical Examiner 1: Yes.

Prosecutor: Please continue.

Medical Examiner 1: Now I start with the... well, first, the next thing I describe is the sharp-force wounds of the hands: There were cutting wounds on the fingers characteristic of the types of wounds we see when it is a defensive injury and someone is trying to grab a sharp instrument before it strikes them somewhere else. There was a cutting wound on the base of the neck, this was not a stab wound, this was longer on the skin surface than it is deep, that's what categorizes it as a cutting wound rather than a stab wound: This was just the left side of the base of the neck: It did have the characteristic sharp end and blunt end: Other than that it was a slit-like defect about 1/8 to 3/16 of an inch deep.

Prosecutor: And when you say a blunt end, characteristic blunt end, and slit end, what does that mean?

Medical Examiner 1: That doesn't identify the knife or sharp implement that caused this wound, but it does tell you that very likely this wound was caused by a type of knife that has a sharp edge and a blunt end, and it doesn't identify a single knife, but it does tell you a little bit about the size of the sharp implement that was used. The next category of wounds that I describe are the sharp-force stab wounds to the chest and abdomen, in particular, I spend a lot of time talking about sharp-force wounds, stab wounds of the left upper chest area. There - there were a total of seven slit-like defects in the skin on the chest and abdomen, total there were seven. But when we did the internal examination of Mr. Johnson's lungs, heart, liver, musculature, and chest cavity walls, I could identify a higher number of wound tracts through the organs than I could identify slit-like defects on the skin surface; so, what I'm trying to say is there were slightly gaping defects in the skin, slit-like defects in the skin, but beneath that opening in the skin there was more than one wound tract, and they met, they intersect, but then they divert: For instance, for one of the stab wounds of the left upper chest we could identify a single slit-like defect in the skin on the skin surface, but we identified five separate wound tracts through the left lung.

Prosecutor: And would that mean that a weapon was not fully removed from the body before it was jammed back in?

Medical Examiner 1: That's one way that that can occur. This... like I say, it was slightly gaping openings in the skin, so it would have been possible to totally withdraw the sharp implement and put it back in the same slit-like defect through the skin.

Judge: If one were to do that, Doctor, would it require some measured act to make sure that it was being inserted in the same area, in your opinion, or would... if I'm thinking about deliberation or a deliberate act, and if you can't, if that's something that you're comfortable answering I understand; but, I understand Mr. Prosecutor's question, and I understand the other alternative you've advanced as well, so I'm just trying to...

Medical Examiner 1: Yeah, I'm not a psychologist. It's hard to understand someone's frame of mind who is doing this. So I don't know what my answer to your question is.

Prosecutor: So, you determined that there was one slit that had potentially five different wounds that would have been created from five separate incidents, if you will?

Medical Examiner 1: We could identify five wound tracts through the left lung and there was a single opening in the skin. I do mention in my description of that would also that there seemed to be a little jagged area along the opening in the skin which might suggest that at one time, there were two slit-like openings in the skin and then either with a total withdrawal of the weapon and another insertion, that little tissue bridge that was in between the two defects in the skin was cut and that's what caused that little jagged edge on the edge of the wound.

Prosecutor: And can you tell me the wound that you just described with the five wound tracts to the lung, would that have proved fatal, that wound alone?

Medical Examiner 1: Well, it would deflate that lung, but if you're asking about just that wound all by itself, it would deflate that lung and there were pulmonary vessels that were transected along those wound tracts, so there would be bleeding into the left chest cavity. It is a wound that you could die from without immediate medical attention. There were two openings in the skin at the left upper chest along that wound tract, one of them did involve severing of a major blood vessel: it involved severing of the subclavian vessel and there was a lot of bleeding associated with the surrounding soft tissue from that. Yeah, It was a transected left subclavian vein, and so there was significant bleeding from that, so that's the left upper chest. There is a wound at the right side of the sternum: That wound path involves the heart. There was a slit-like defect right at the base of the aorta, and considerable bleeding from that wound into the pericardial sack.

Medical Examiner 1: There is another wound at the left side of the sternum that also injures the heart and the thoracic aorta; so again, there's more bleeding into the left chest cavity and the pericardial sack. There are two wounds actually that are on the right side of the lower chest and upper abdomen area: Those wounds involve the liver, and again with these wound tracts it was difficult to say exactly the number of times the wound tracts were there because there was a section of the liver where you couldn't identify a tract any more: The tissue was so badly damaged it was .. I don't describe it that way, but it was like pulpified, and so we lost the ability to talk about tracts that went through there because it wasn't a tract anymore, it was just liver tissue that was like pulp.

Prosecutor: Would that be indicative of multiple, multiple penetrations in that area?

Medical Examiner 1: It could be: It could also be a motion of the sharp implement while it's still inside the body. We could identify an endpoint for some of these wounds: For instance, the top of the right kidney was injured twice, and there is a large muscle that is supportive of our back and lower spine called the psoas muscle that had slit-like defects in it, and there were two that we could identify, and I thought that I had identified all the wound tracts through that area, but then I noted there were two additional slit-like defects of the psoas muscle kind of down lower further inferior from that. So from those two openings in the skin, there was a minimum of four tracts through the liver and kidney, and one there was an injury to the pancreas and the psoas muscle.

Prosecutor: And were you able to tell anything from the two slit-like openings that produced those four wound tracts? Previously you had indicated that in the other slit-like opening further up on the body it's possible the knife could have been removed, or the object, whatever it may be, stabbing implement and put back in because of the jagged edges that you could see, did you find that here?

Medical Examiner 1: Yes, but for the reason I described before, these wounds were not as gaping as the wounds on the left upper chest, and so my thought was, since there was this area of extreme damage to the liver, my thought was that there was more motion of the implement while It was still inside the body and, you know, not complete withdrawal.

Prosecutor: Okay. Would there have to be some withdrawal?

Medical Examiner 1: Yes.

Prosecutor: So what did you see?

Medical Examiner 1: Yes, just to redirect the angle of the implementation. There were stab wounds on the right side of the chest and the abdominal cavity, and one stab wound on the left side of the abdomen: This one, in particular, exposed some of the intestinal tract, and that was something that was noted at the scene was that a small segment of the small intestine had exited and was externalized through that wound at the scene. And the next set of injuries that I describe are just some minor superficial contusions and abrasions of the lower extremities, a contusion of the shin, I believe it was on the right, and some abrasions of the knees, over bony prominences of the knees.

Prosecutor: Okay, and is that the sum and substance of the injuries that you found?

Medical Examiner 1: That concludes my description of the injuries. These are standard descriptions of the sharp force wounds: They do include my estimation of wound depth, so, you know... and some of them, because there were slit-like defects on, you know, the chest cavity well or in the case of the psoas muscle, I estimated that some of the stab wounds, like for instance the ones involving the liver and the psoas muscle, they had a depth of up to, you know, seven to nine inches.

Prosecutor: Okay. I don't know if you can answer this or not, but of the injuries that you found, how many of those injuries would prove fatal on their own if you can answer?

Medical Examiner 1: Without treatment, the sharp-force wounds that involved the heart could be rapidly fatal, not only because of the blood loss but because they involve areas of the heart that could involve the conduction system, and they would upset the regular heart rhythm, the beating of the heart and stop it that way. Where there were defects in the heart, there were also defects in the overlying pericardia sack, so this wasn't a case of what we call tamponade, where the pericardial sack fills up with blood and stops the heart from beating properly because of the pressure because there were openings in the pericardial sack as well, so the blood was able to leak out into the chest cavities and the abdominal cavity once the diaphragm was injured. So, out of the seven openings of the skin, I would say at least four of those, because of the injuries to the lungs, the bleeding from the injury to the liver, and injuries to the heart, I would say at least four of them would be rapidly fatal all by themselves.

Prosecutor: And you have documented several, I guess, stab-type wounds: How many wound tracts do you think you found?

Medical Examiner 1: A minimum of 16.

Prosecutor: And what was the total number of stab wounds? Was that seven?

Medical Examiner 1: Well, there were seven openings in the skin, seven slit-like defects in the skin.

Prosecutor: Producing 16 wound tracts?

Medical Examiner 1: But the tracts that we identified, there's a minimum of 16.

Prosecutor: Okay. Looking at the number and the type of wounds overall that Mr. Johnson sustained, can you draw any conclusions as to what type of incident he was involved in based on the type of injuries and the number of injuries? I mean, this was a violent occurrence?

Judge: Are you asking does she has an opinion as to the manner of death?

Prosecutor: Well, I guess that's not quite the root of my question yet. And if you can't answer that question, it doesn't make sense.

Medical Examiner: I'm not sure. I describe injuries. I can't know what was in the mind of Mr. Johnson or his assailant while this was going on.

Prosecutor: Okay. Now, based upon your autopsy, were you able to determine the cause of death?

Medical Examiner 1: Yes. I stated the cause of death as sharp-force wounds of the chest and abdomen: there was a contributory cause of blunt-impact head trauma.

Prosecutor: And were you able to determine the manner of death of Mr. Johnson?

Medical Examiner 1: The manner of death is homicide.

Prosecutor: Doctor, regarding the contributing cause of blunt-impact head trauma, would the head trauma have contributed to death or could it have on its own caused death?

Medical Examiner 1: He didn't have contusions of his brain, he did not have significant bleeding around his brain in terms of, you know, subarachnoid or subdural hemorrhage, and his brain did not appear to be swollen: So, without an injury to the brain, the head trauma all by itself at the most it would be a concussive-type injury which would cause a temporary altering of consciousness, which, you know, again, we look at small tissue samples under a microscope to see if we can see changes in the cells that would indicate hypoxia or injury of some sort; he did not have that: What that means is that these injuries were acquired in a period that was rapid enough so that those changes in his brain cells did not occur.

Prosecutor: Do you have any idea what generally that period would be for those changes in brain cells to occur?

Medical Examiner 1: No, I don't.

Prosecutor: And so there would be no way then to tell the length of any kind of altercation or violent encounter that he was involved in based upon just looking at the injuries and being able to determine the time between each injury and when it occurred?

Medical Examiner 1: I don't know the order of wounds, I think I mentioned before that there are wounds that have characteristics that possibly happened early on in his assault, and to say that because they have soft tissue injury with, like with edema that kind of indicates that he had a higher blood pressure or, you know, closer-to-normal blood pressure when that wound was inflicted. There are some of the scalp lacerations that don't show vital change in the soft tissue around the wound at all, they almost look like they could have been inflicted post-mortem. So, that's the only thing that I can describe that would help to tell us, when, based on these findings this injury occurred before this one. But you know, that's the best I can do for giving a timeline for how these injuries occurred.

Prosecutor: Okay. Thank you, Doctor. I don't have anything further.

Judge: Thank you, Medical Examiner 1. You're excused.

Chapter 25: Forensic Psychologist 1

Judge: Mr. Prosecutor, do the People have any other evidence to offer today to assist this court in determining whether or not there is support for finding that the defendant has committed the acts the State has charged her with?

Prosecutor: I have no other evidence to submit today, your Honor.

Judge: Mr. Prosecutor, and it's your belief, that the evidence that has been received thus far, both testimonial and by way of an exhibit, establishes support that the defendant has committed the crimes that she's been charged with?

Prosecutor: Yes, Your Honor, that's correct.

Judge: Does the defense as well?

Defense Council: We acknowledge that, Your Honor, yes.

Judge: And that's the first prong of Michigan court Rule 6.3041C11. Now, Ms. Defense Council, do you intend to introduce any evidence that demonstrates that your client may have been legally insane at the time that these crimes were committed?

Defense Council: I do, Your Honor. I will testify Forensic Psychologist 1, the forensic psychologist who conducted the criminal responsibility evaluation, as well as that of Forensic Psychologist 2, who was retained by the Prosecution to conduct an independent evaluation. I also, your Honor, have a notebook that has been marked as Defendant's Exhibit D that contains the bulk of the incident reports that were gathered and compiled by Detective Sergeant 2: By stipulation of the parties, I would move for the admission of these documents into evidence in further support of both the fact that the crime was committed and that the defendant committed it, and also in support of a finding that she was insane at the time.

Judge: Defendant's Exhibit D contains the respective police reports and other documents that, by stipulation, the parties asked that I receive and review last week, is that correct?

Defense Council: That is correct, your Honor, and we're offering it by way of supplementation to the testimony that the court has already heard.

Judge: Defendant's Exhibit D is received by stipulation, and just so that the record is clear and those who are here understand, Forensic Psychologist 1, Mr. Prosecutor, was the initial doctor tasked with reviewing and evaluating the defendant's relative to criminal responsibility under an order of the court, is that correct?

Prosecutor: That is correct.

Judge: And that initial evaluation was ordered to be conducted by the Center for Forensic Psychiatry and it's Forensic Psychologist 1 who was tasked with that responsibility, correct?

Prosecutor: That is correct.

Judge: After the parties received Forensic Psychologist 1's report, you, on behalf of the State, then elected to seek an independent evaluation.

Prosecutor: I did, Your Honor.

Judge: And that independent evaluation was performed by Forensic Psychologist 2?

Prosecutor: Yes.

Judge: The defense has not sought and obtained their own independent expert's opinion relative to criminal responsibility: You rely solely upon the Center for Forensic Psychiatry's doctor's opinion, Doctor's opinion, as well as the independent evaluation that the state sought out and obtained by Forensic Psychologist 2?

Defense Council: That is correct, Your Honor.

Judge: The doctors will be called by the defense?

Defense Council: That is correct, your Honor, and with the court's permission I do need some time. We'd originally subpoenaed the doctors for this afternoon, but matters have moved more quickly than anticipated. They're on call so I do need some time to let them know that we are ready for them. Also, by the court's request, we will be doing a dry run to make sure that the technology is in order.

Judge: Just tell me when you're ready. We'll be in recess.

Clerk: (Recess taken at 10:09 a.m. Back on record at 10:40 a.m.)

Judge: Ms. Defense Council, do you have a witness?

Defense Council: I do, Your Honor, Forensic Psychologist 1, who will be appearing by Zoom here this morning.

Judge: Good morning, Sir. Are you Forensic Psychologist 1?

Defense Council: It was just working.

Judge: I'll recess for a moment. When he is in the room, don't put him in a waiting room. Let's get our technology in order.

Clerk: (Recess taken at 10:41 a.m... Back on record at 10:55 a.m.)

Judge: As counsel knows, our supreme court, shortly after the COVID-19 pandemic had taken hold in this country and this state, passed several local administrative orders that have now been modified by court rule that requires the court to use virtual means whenever possible to allow remote witnesses to appear and provide testimony; unfortunately, this seems to be more of the norm than the exception, meaning the challenge of having someone appear virtually. As I understand Forensic Psychologist 1, he may not be an employee of the center for Forensic Psychiatry but he has authored the report as a contract doctor for the center, is that correct, Mr. Prosecutor?

Prosecutor: That's my understanding.

Judge: Do you agree?

Defense Council: That's my understanding.

Judge: The Center for Forensic Psychiatry can use the Polycom system as does this court and avoid appearing through Zoom, which then creates additional technological issues. Ms. Defense Council, because you're calling Forensic Psychologist 1, I would suggest that you touch base with him and have him immediately report to the Center for Forensic Psychiatry and attempt to utilize the Polycom system with this court if he cannot ensure a connection through Zoom in a meaningful way.

Judge: It's incredibly disrespectful to the families that are here, to the attorneys, to Ms. Ross, and to the court if that's not going to be something that can occur. The second doctor, Forensic Psychologist 2, can appear virtually and must be tested before we can continue this hearing. So, what I would propose is that we continue this matter until 1:00 to give you some time, Ms. Defense Council, to logistically discuss with Dr. Forensic Psychologist 1 how he will appear and provide meaningful testimony virtually. I think and I believe by Polycom at the center would be the most appropriate way, but I'll leave that up to you and your witness, and you should also ensure Forensic Psychologist 2 ability to participate virtually.

Defense Council: Yes, Your Honor.

Judge: So, any objection to proceeding in that way, Mr. Prosecutor?

Prosecutor: No, Your Honor.

Defense Council: No, Your Honor.

Judge: Then we will be in recess until 1:00, where I will expect to hear a witness.

Clerk: (Recess taken at 10:58 a.m. Back on record at 12:54 p.m.)

Judge: Ms. Defense Council, do you have a witness?

Defense Council: I do, your Honor, at this time, I would call Forensic Psychologist 1, who is present by Zoom.

Judge: Doctor, can you hear me?

Forensic Psychologist 1: Yes, I can.

Judge: I'm Judge (REDACTED). Doctor, our clerk is going to place you under oath.

Clerk: Would you please raise your right hand? Do you solemnly swear or affirm that any testimony you give in this case will be the truth, the whole truth, and nothing but the truth, so help you God?

Forensic Psychologist 1: I do.

Defense Council: Doctor, can you see me?

Forensic Psychologist 1: Yes, I can.

Defense Council: Okay. I'm (REDACTED), counsel for the defendant in this matter, as you are most likely aware. First please, state your name and spell it for the record.

Forensic Psychologist 1: (REDACTED)

Defense Council: And what is your occupation?

Forensic Psychologist 1: Forensic Psychologist.

Defense Council: And for whom do you work?

Forensic Psychologist 1: Center for Forensic Psychiatry, State of Michigan, Department of Health and Human Services.

Defense Council: Are you, in fact, then a licensed psychologist in the State of Michigan?

Forensic Psychologist 1: Yes, licensed psychologist and a certified consulting forensic examiner.

Defense Council: And how long have you been licensed?

Forensic Psychologist 1: Since 2014.

Defense Council: Can you tell us a bit about your educational background?

Forensic Psychologist 1: Sure. I earned a bachelor's degree in psychology from (REDACTED) in 2006, then I earned a master of counseling and a doctorate in clinical psychology from (REDACTED) in 2013, completed a pre-doctoral internship at (REDACTED), post-doctoral internship at (REDACTED), got my license and have since been employed at the center for Forensic Psychiatry.

Defense Council: Are you employed anywhere else?

Forensic Psychologist 1: I have a standing credential as an adjunct clinical instructor with (REDACTED) as it relates to providing training and supervision to psychiatry residents and fellows who are at the center, as well as new psychologists and psychiatrists for supervising and teaching didactic seminars here at the center.

Defense Council: In the course of your work for the Forensic Center, Doctor, what types of things do you do?

Forensic Psychologist 1: Primarily I conduct competency to stand trial and criminal responsibility evaluations: I also serve on a committee from privileging and credentialing, and I teach seminars and supervise trainees and psychiatric fellows.

Defense Council: And do you have an idea about how many evaluations for criminal responsibility you've done?

Forensic Psychologist 1: Yeah, I've done about 900 forensic evaluations and approximately 530 criminal responsibility evaluations.

Defense Council: And have you been qualified as an expert in a court of law previously?

Forensic Psychologist 1: Yes, I have.

Defense Council: Now, Doctor, would you please describe to us what it means to conduct a criminal responsibility evaluation?

Forensic Psychologist 1: Sure. So a criminal responsibility evaluation is initiated by court order to evaluation in which, as a forensic examiner, I evaluate a defendant for purposes of giving an opinion about whether I think they meet the statutory definition for legal insanity, which has to do with one's mental state at the time of an alleged offense: To do that evaluation I see the person, these days either in person or via video conference like we are doing here in the courtroom. I can review the police report, have an interview

MY FATHER'S STORY

with the defendant in which I review their background history and the alleged offense and get their account of it, review what's in the police report, and then I also receive and review as many collateral records as I can obtain about the person's treatment history, medical, psychiatric, things of that nature.

Defense Council: Doctor, in this instance, did you have occasion to evaluate Ms. Angelee Ross for criminal responsibility?

Forensic Psychologist 1: Yes I did.

Defense Council: And did you author a report?

Forensic Psychologist 1: I did.

Defense Council: And do you recall the date of that report?

Forensic Psychologist 1: The report was submitted on July 23rd, 2021.

Defense Council: And there was an addendum made a little later, correct?

Forensic Psychologist 1: Yes. The addendum was dated October 20th, 2021.

Defense Council: And what was the purpose of that addendum?

Forensic Psychologist 1: I had made a minor factual error about who informed the police about something Ms. Ross had told them in the time leading up to the alleged accident.

Defense Council: Okay. In the course of conducting the criminal responsibility evaluation for Ms. Ross can you tell us what steps you took?

Forensic Psychologist 1: Sure. So first, we receive the order and schedule the evaluation. I saw her via video conference from the jail, and before seeing her I reviewed all three available police reports from Michigan State Police, Cadillac Police Department, and the Manistee County Sheriff's office, as well as the 911 communications records and the audio recordings. I spoke with her in the interview, as I said, about background history: It was also just about any pertinent background information that I was able to obtain. I reviewed the police report with her, I got a detailed account from her of her account of the alleged offense and the time surrounding it, and we discussed any discrepancies or any clarifications that she had related to the police report. Then I also obtained records from various mental health and medical facilities that I reviewed and put all of that information together to integrate it into an opinion about the legal insanity criteria.

Defense Council: And what was your opinion?

Forensic Psychologist 1: It was my opinion Ms. Ross met the criteria for legal insanity at the time.

Defense Council: Can you tell us, please, what that means?

Forensic Psychologist 1: Sure. Well, it's my understanding that the legal insanity statute indicates that a criminal defendant is considered legally insane if, because of an intellectual disability or mental illness, that person lacks substantial capacity to appreciate the nature and quality, or the wrongfulness of their actions, or to conform their actions to the law's requirements.

Defense Council: And again, not to be too repetitive, you concluded that she satisfied that definition?

Forensic Psychologist 1: Correct.

Defense Council: And those conclusions are contained in the report that we just mentioned?

Forensic Psychologist 1: They are.

Defense Council: Was there anything particularly unusual about this evaluation process, Doctor?

Forensic Psychologist 1: No, it was pretty standard.

Defense Council: And in your opinion, was this conclusion that you reached a close call?

Forensic Psychologist 1: No. As far as forensically speaking it was very clear, in my opinion.

Defense Council: Okay. Thank you. I have nothing further.

Prosecutor: Doctor, this is Mr. Prosecutor. Can you hear me okay?

Forensic Psychologist 1: Yes, I can.

Prosecutor: So, doctor, when and where did the examination take place of Ms. Ross when you did your interview?

Forensic Psychologist 1: It took place on May 26th, 2021, via video conference in the custody of the jail.

Prosecutor: Do you know how long the interview was?

Forensic Psychologist 1: My records show one hour and thirty minutes.

Prosecutor: Okay. Ms. Defense Council had previously asked you about your report, and you have authored a report that's been entered into evidence, I did want to ask you a couple of questions about that report. Doctor, on page 3 of your report, you discuss Ms. Ross describing her severe mental deterioration, she also believed the purge was coming, satellites were spying on her from inside her home, and the people out to get her were striking the electric grid sending her messages to prove her worth so she would not be killed in the purge. Was it your understanding that she currently had those beliefs while she was being interviewed, or she was relaying to you what she had believed at the time?

Forensic Psychologist 1: She was relaying to me what she believed at the time, and she did not report believing that at the time that we were speaking.

Prosecutor: Would you have attributed that to anything, any antipsychotic medications that she was on? I see your report indicates that she was on Zyprexa: Would that have any effect on that, on those beliefs?

Forensic Psychologist 1: Yeah. Based on the evidence, in my opinion, that she was experiencing psychotic symptoms at the time and was not on any medication, the Zyprexa and any other antipsychotic medication tend to be effective at mitigating those symptoms.

Prosecutor: Is there ever a situation where maybe somebody is on Zyprexa and those symptoms are mitigated, but after a while, they could return while that person is still on that medication such that it may have to be changed or altered?

Forensic Psychologist 1: Well, just for clarification, I'm not a psychiatrist, and so the effects of specific medications and interactions are not my expertise. So I don't want to say for certain because I can't speak to that, but, you know, I can tell you that each person is different, and each person's biology may interact differently with certain medications, so it is possible.

Prosecutor: And in your experience, Doctor, if you can answer this question, I realize you're not an M.D. or a psychiatrist, but if somebody who was experiencing symptoms went on the Zyprexa and those symptoms at least somewhat abated, if they were to go off the Zyprexa, is there any telling what would happen?

Forensic Psychologist 1: Typically, the symptoms would return. If somebody has a psychotic disorder and it's symptomatic and then becomes less symptomatic on the medication, it's not uncommon for those symptoms to return.

Prosecutor: Doctor, is malingering something that you were trying to look for?

Forensic Psychologist 1: It's something that's always on my radar and does occasionally occur in the forensic world of examinations.

Prosecutor: And what kind of things do you look for to determine whether or not somebody may be malingering?

Forensic Psychologist 1: Well, I look for... well, first of all, I have expertise in understanding what an authentic psychotic disorder looks like, so if a person is reporting symptoms or experiences that are not consistent with that, that would raise a flag. I also look for consistency of cross-collateral records, so, you know, what a defendant or any person tells me is one source of the information that I hold, and then I'm also looking across other accounts, in this case, the police report and various medical records all documented the same observations or similar, and that's over some time, so in this particular case all the information was consistent, and so I didn't have any reason to believe that there was any feigning or exaggeration of any symptoms.

Prosecutor: And how does a previous mental health history factor into that analysis? Does that factor in?

Forensic Psychologist 1: I'm sorry, can you repeat the last part of your question?

Prosecutor: Yes. Does a previous mental health history factor into not only your examination but also any potential exaggeration or malingering?

Forensic Psychologist 1: It certainly could. I look at whatever records are available: In Ms. Ross' case, I think they dated back to 2019, and so I would look to see, you know, how that person presented at the time of those records and, you know, how they responded to any, you know, treatment or interaction with others, and again look at the consistency and any patterns that emerge.

Prosecutor: If somebody is experiencing a psychotic episode, would it be uncommon to be drifting potentially in and out of what would appear to be conscious or extremely tired? Is that a usual symptom either during or after a psychotic episode?

Forensic Psychologist 1: It can be. Psychotic symptoms vary. They could be what would be considered negative symptoms, meaning sort of a lack or loss of behavior in which a person is either staring or appear to be losing consciousness or be internally distracted and not really in tune with what's happening around them in the external environment, or they could be more positive symptoms which would be more actively behavioral symptoms, you know, making bizarre statements, expressing beliefs that aren't based in reality, acting in bizarre ways, so they could take any number of those forms.

Prosecutor: And what is - what is your diagnosis, if you made one, of Ms. Ross's mental illness? What is the mental illness that you found?

Forensic Psychologist 1: So I don't do specific diagnoses in my evaluation, but based on the records that I reviewed, if I had to give an opinion on what I think would be most consistent it would be something akin to Schizophrenia.

Prosecutor: And would that be considered a mental illness within the State of Michigan, the laws of the State of Michigan?

Forensic Psychologist 1: Yeah. I mean, the state, as I understand it, doesn't it defines a mental illness as a substantial thought or mood disorder that significantly impairs one's functioning or ability to recognize reality, and that would meet that definition in my opinion.

Prosecutor: And her symptoms, do you believe the symptoms she exhibited at the time of this incident would meet that definition?

Forensic Psychologist 1: In my opinion, yes.

Prosecutor: What would cause? I know you're familiar with the facts of this case, what could cause somebody to have this type of episode?

Forensic Psychologist 1: Well, that's a good question and the research doesn't have a specific, you know, one-to-one conclusion or understanding of what exactly causes a psychotic disorder; it appears to be some combination of genetic predisposition and environmental stressors that, you know, can lead a person to experience these types of symptoms: It does have a strong genetic component across generations although you don't always see that. In some cases, it can be exacerbated or precipitated by substance use, which I didn't have evidence of in this particular case. But the short answer is that there's not one understanding of why or how it develops.

Prosecutor: So we may not understand what all the triggers are, or more specifically what one person's triggers are?

Forensic Psychologist 1: Right. We can put the information together based on what we have. There was not one particular cause as I'm aware.

Prosecutor: All right. And so, would there be any way to predict whether one of those episodes could happen again with an individual patient or person?

Forensic Psychologist 1: Well, I would say it's not possible to predict anything in the future with certainty, but what I can say is that individuals with a psychotic disorder that is a bona fide disorder as indicated by, you know, personal history and records and things like that, it tends to be a life-long illness, and so those symptoms do remit if the person is not on treatment that is shown to be helpful.

Prosecutor: Okay. If you'll bear with me, Doctor, just one second. And Doctor, you concluded that Ms. Ross lacks substantial capacity to appreciate the nature and quality, or the wrongfulness of her conduct: What went into that? What did you use to come to that conclusion specifically?

Forensic Psychologist 1: Yeah. So, I used the information in the police report and the records that documented multiple people related to her, including the decedent and her son and others including the decedent's former boss who indicated to police that she was making bizarre statements related to the purge and all the other things alluded in the report. In the weeks surrounding the alleged incident, she also contacted 911 on multiple occasions expressing the same bizarre delusions, and the reasoning that she gave after her arrest when she was interviewed by the police also was consistent with the same information, and when she was in the hospital after her arrest prior to, I believe, being taken to jail she was also acting bizarrely, and all of those things lead me to believe, based on what she was saying and how she was acting, that she wasn't aware of exactly what was going on or, you know, the nature of what her actions were. Specifically, she did indicate in the police report that she committed the murder, but her reasonings for doing so when asked and all the other behavior was not based on reality; so it was my opinion that, although she knew that she had killed this individual, the reasons for doing so and her actions at the time were not consistent with somebody who was based in reality.

Prosecutor: Is it common for someone who is experiencing a psychotic episode to kind of fixate on an issue, for instance, in this case, a purge, and to repeatedly talk about that issue, is that common?

Forensic Psychologist 1: Yes, it does happen.

Prosecutor: Okay. Thank you. I don't have anything further of this witness.

Judge: Doctor, you have testified that, although you do not diagnose a mental illness, you believe that, based upon your review, Ms. Ross suffers from something akin to...is it Paranoia Schizophrenia?

Forensic Psychologist 1: Schizophrenia. It may be one of the qualifiers, but I'm not sure. I would say paranoid is a fair modifier, yes.

Judge: In your report, you describe a psychotic disorder: Is it a psychotic break or a psychotic episode, is that one way in which someone who suffers from schizophrenia may appear?

Forensic Psychologist 1: Yes. It's a hallmark of the disorder.

Judge: Are there any other traits that someone who suffers from Schizophrenia may exhibit, that you're aware of?

Forensic Psychologist 1: Yeah. Well, so a psychotic disorder such as Schizophrenia tends to be episodic, and so when a person is in an acute psychotic state, their behavior would be more bizarre and pronounced, such as what we see in this case at this time; otherwise, they may be functioning well at times. They're typically more symptomatic when not on medication if medication is shown to be helpful. Other symptoms can include more discrete or less obvious things such as difficulty with social engagement, you know, and low ability to understand what's going on in interaction with somebody or with their environment. They may attribute special personalized meanings of things that are not associated or based on reality, for example, associate particular numbers with certain meanings, they may feel as though they receive personalized messages from something like a television show or the radio.

Judge: Could they receive a personalized message from an animal, for example?

Forensic Psychologist 1: Sure, it's possible.

Judge: You described being aware, during your evaluation for criminal responsibility, that Ms. Ross had been prescribed Zyprexa and Buspar: Was it your understanding that she was currently receiving those medications at the time that you evaluated her?

Forensic Psychologist 1: I don't believe so.

Judge: I'm reading from page 3 of the report and it would be the second full paragraph: "Ms. Ross' mental state has grown more stable since consistently taking prescribed antipsychotics Zyprexa and anxiety Buspar medications." And really, where I'm going with this, Doctor did you perform not only the criminal responsibility evaluation, but did you perform an earlier competency to stand trial evaluation or did a different doctor?

Forensic Psychologist 1: Let me confirm that. I'm not sure if she was ever referred for a competency examination.

Defense Council: She was referred for a competency evaluation.

Forensic Psychologist 1: It may have been me. Let me confirm, I apologize because it would have been prior and I have the records here.

Judge: What I'm trying to establish is competency was raised when this matter was in the district court before it was bound over to the circuit court, and counsel, if you can tell me, was she required to undergo a regimen of medication, including Zyprexa and Buspar to restore her to competency?

Defense Council: Not by anyone from the Forensic center, but by the jail clinician, I believe, as the treating physician for her.

Judge: But the jail clinician wasn't doing that under a court order to restore her to competency?

Prosecutor: That's correct, Your Honor.

Defense Council: And, for the record, Your Honor, the competency evaluation, due to some scheduling issues, actually took place after the criminal responsibility: I believe the report is dated July 29th.

Forensic Psychologist 1: I have it pulled up. I apologize for the miscommunication, but I believe that is consistent with what I have.

Judge: All right. Thank you, Doctor. I don't have any other questions. Thank you, sir.

Chapter 26: Forensic Psychologist 2

Judge: Ms. Defense Council, please call your next witness.

Defense Council: Thank you. At this time, I would call Forensic Psychologist 2, who is present and appearing by video conferencing.

Judge: Good afternoon, Doctor. Can you hear me?

Forensic Psychologist 2: Yes, Your Honor.

Judge: Doctor, our clerk is going to place you under oath.

Clerk: Would you please raise your right hand? Do you solemnly swear or affirm that any testimony you give in this case will be the truth, the whole truth, and nothing but the truth, so help you God?

Forensic Psychologist 2: Yes, I do.

Defense Council: Doctor, would you please state your name and spell it for the record?

Forensic Psychologist 2: (REDACTED)

Defense Council: And what is your occupation?

Forensic Psychologist 2: I work in private practice as a forensic psychologist conducting psychological evaluations of criminal defendants.

Defense Council: And how long have you been doing that work?

Forensic Psychologist 2: I've been doing this for 20 years. I started at the Center for Forensic Psychiatry, worked there until 2006, and have worked in an independent practice doing the same thing for the past 16 years.

Defense Council: Can you tell us a little bit about your educational background, please?

Forensic Psychologist 2: Yes. I have a bachelor's degree in psychology from (REDACTED), a master's degree in experimental psychology, and a Ph.D. in clinical psychology from (REDACTED). I'm fully licensed in the State of Michigan.

Defense Council: Thank you, Doctor. In addition to your credentials and your work experience, it appears, according to your CV, that you have significant advanced training in forensic psychology, would that be fair to state?

Forensic Psychologist 2: Yes. I've participated in continuing education programs in the area of forensic psychology.

Defense Council: Doctor, have you done numerous criminal responsibility evaluations throughout your career?

Forensic Psychologist 2: Yes, I've conducted evaluations of, I think it's approaching 3,000 criminal defendants, the majority are likely evaluations of criminal responsibility both when I worked at the Forensic Center and in independent practice.

Defense Council: And have you been qualified as an expert in a court of law previously?

Forensic Psychologist 2: Yes, I've testified as a clinical and forensic psychologist over 200 times in state and federal courts.

Defense Council: Okay. In this particular matter, Doctor, you were initially retained by the Prosecution, correct?

Forensic Psychologist 2: Yes.

Defense Council: And what was the purpose of that retention?

Forensic Psychologist 2: I spoke with the Prosecutor, the attorney from the Prosecuting attorney's office, and he informed me that there was a case that the Forensic Center had determined met the criteria for legal insanity, and he wanted another set of eyes on it, so he referred it for an independent evaluation for me to review the case, meet with the defendant, and advise him of my opinion on the facts of the case.

Defense Council: And you did do that, correct?

Forensic Psychologist 2: Yes, I did.

Defense Council: And can you tell us what you did to make your evaluation or conduct your evaluation?

Forensic Psychologist 2: So I'll tell you the procedures that I engaged in to conduct the evaluation. What I did was what I generally do in a criminal responsibility evaluation, it involves obtaining information from a variety of sources. What I had, in this case, was a great deal of discovery materials in terms of the police reports, witness statements, over four hours of recordings of interactions with the defendant, but also 911 calls and interviews of some other witnesses. I conducted a three-hour meeting with the defendant in the county jail, part of that was a clinical interview, and part of that was the administration of psychological testing. So then, once I gathered all the information, I analyzed the testing and tried to synthesize the materials to determine the relative components of a criminal responsibility opinion in terms of whether she was mentally ill at the time and what effect that illness had on her behavior.

Defense Council: And did you conclude?

Forensic Psychologist 2: Yes, I did.

MY FATHER'S STORY

Defense Council: And what was your conclusion, Doctor?

Forensic Psychologist 2: In consultation with the retaining attorney, I described there's a strong basis for a finding that Ms. Ross suffers from a severe mental illness and there is convincing information to support my conclusion that the symptoms of her condition were worsening during the time leading up to the crimes. Particularly powerful were the 911 calls before the crimes, and then the observations of her behavior both by the arresting officers and her behavior in the jail. All of this leads me to offer the opinion that she did suffer from a substantial disorder of thought and mood during the time in question and would be considered mentally ill. Well, the next step was determining whether her mental illness affected her appreciation of nature and quality, or her behavior, and her appreciation for the wrongfulness of her conduct, and it was my opinion after analyzing the facts of the case that there was no reality-based motivation for this behavior and that her thoughts and behavior were grossly disorganized and influenced by a psychosis in that she was experiencing delusional beliefs that were both paranoid and delusions of reference.

Forensic Psychologist 2: Delusions of reference involve a belief that benign or random events have a specific meaning or are sent as messages to this person, but she also had the paranoia that guided her behavior, and as I said, the 911 calls where she's asking for help and appearing very desperate were very strong evidence in my analysis, and the fact that others recognized that she was having severe mental health problems during the time supported that conclusion as well. The next step is that, because of these delusional beliefs and disorganized thoughts, it was unable to confirm her conduct to the requirements of the law, so I thought that the available information supported a finding of legal insanity.

Defense Council: Thank you, Doctor. And did you author a one-page report that you submitted to the Prosecuting Attorney?

Forensic Psychologist 2: Yes, I did.

Defense Council: Okay, and is that report dated January 27th, 2022?

Forensic Psychologist 2: Yes, it is.

Defense Council: Doctor, I think you've made yourself very clear, but just to be even more clear in layman's terms, was this a close call?

Forensic Psychologist 2: It's my opinion that this was not a close call and that there's very strong support for a finding of legal insanity. I considered alternative hypotheses in that I believe I left no stone unturned trying to get to the bottom of this, and in my opinion, this is a very strong finding for that she was unable to appreciate the nature and quality, or the wrongfulness of her actions and conform her behavior because of the severe and acute symptoms that she experienced during that time.

Defense Council: Thank you, Doctor. I have no further questions.

Prosecutor: I have some questions. Good afternoon, Doctor. It's the Prosecutor here. I know you probably can't see me. I'm at the podium, and I hope it's okay if I ask you questions from this location.

Forensic Psychologist 2: Yes, sir. I can hear you.

Prosecutor: Very good. Now, Doctor, you administered psychological testing, basically an assessment inventory, what does that consist of?

Forensic Psychologist 2: A personality assessment inventory is a self-report questionnaire consisting of 344 items: It provides information about two primary areas: The first is it has validity scales to address whether a person is exaggerating or minimizing symptoms of mental illness, and that is often a very important piece of information a criminal responsibility evaluation. For this defendant, there were no signs that she was exaggerating or minimizing symptoms of mental illness and it was determined that testing was a reliable measure of her true mental status. The other part is the clinical scales which show what problem areas a person has and the severity of these problem areas relative to other people in the population. Her clinical scales testing identified severe problems in the areas of mood disorder, anxiety, and psychosis, which was consistent with the treatment record and her presentation and the description in the police reports: So, all these data points were consistent in showing that she is a person who suffers from mental illness, but it showed that her mental illness occurs in the absence of a substance abuse which was another factor that I considered, but testing did not identify problem in the areas of substance abuse.

Prosecutor: Now you had talked about the first part of that test and it almost sounds like it's designed to test for malingering, or exaggeration, or faking of symptoms, is that correct?

Forensic Psychologist 2: Well, it can provide that type of information toward a conclusion about malingering and also minimization of symptoms which occurs sometimes: In this case, it was probably helpful in determining the absence of malingering as far as the testing was concerned. But malingering is not determined just by one test, it's by a consistency between the symptoms as described from a variety of different data points, and I think the testing results are supportive of the overall finding that is a valid case of mental illness; it's not, in my opinion, malingering was considered and ruled out.

Prosecutor: Do you have a diagnosis of her mental condition?

Forensic Psychologist 2: Well, I think that there is a very likely diagnosis, and what we're looking at here is three primary components of her mental illness: The first is a mood disorder in terms of severe episodes of depression, but also mania where her energy levels and mood fluctuate greatly when she's in such an episode: The other part involves anxiety, but her anxiety is tied to the paranoia which is the other main component of psychosis. So, with the combination of psychosis and mood disorder, you've looking at two primary diagnoses that this could be: The first is a bipolar disorder with psychotic features, which I think is the most likely diagnosis because it has psychotic symptoms that occur during episodes of severe mood disturbance whether it's mania or depression. The other possible diagnosis is schizoaffective disorder bipolar type: The main difference between this is, in schizoaffective disorder, the psychotic symptoms can persist even when there's no severe depression or mania, and the differentiation between these two diagnoses comes after looking at her adjustment over long periods, whether her psychosis persists when she's depressed or manic. But I think that the most likely diagnosis and the best characterization of her mental state is a bipolar disorder with psychotic features.

Prosecutor: Is there a prognosis for recovery of someone with that condition, or is that a life-long condition that someone must deal with?

Forensic Psychologist 2: Well, it is a lifelong condition. There are effective treatments for this condition, primarily or initially in the form of psychotropic medications: There are mood-stabilizing medications and antipsychotic medications that can be effective in addressing the primary symptoms: If this is coupled with psychotherapy where a person learns to manage their symptoms and recognize triggers of the onset of a new episode and rely upon treatment providers, this is a condition then can be effectively managed as long as the person maintains medication treatment; if the person were to discontinue treatment with medication, we would expect a relapse of symptoms.

Prosecutor: Is there any guarantee if someone is on a course of treatment or medication that, they would not relapse into a psychotic episode?

Forensic Psychologist 2: I'm sorry, would you repeat the question, please?

Prosecutor: So if a patient is undergoing a course of treatment medication, that is whether it's Zyprexa or some other antipsychotic medication, is there any guarantee that while they're on that medication, they couldn't experience a psychotic episode, that is to say, if somebody is medicated could they still experience a psychotic episode depending on what's going on?

Forensic Psychologist 2: Yes, sometimes certain medications can become less effective over time, and the person can experience increasing symptoms which often leads to a switch in medication. There's a variety of antipsychotic medications that can be effective, and if a person continues to experience symptoms on one medication, their psychiatrist can change the treatment program until these are alleviated.

Prosecutor: And would it be common for somebody who manages symptoms through medication, if they were to go off that medication, would it be common to experience a psychotic episode?

Forensic Psychologist 2: Yes. That would be the case, if the person were to discontinue treatment there's no guarantee that they would experience those symptoms, but there is a high probability that they might relapse with some symptoms or have a subsequent episode in the absence of treatment; that's why this must be a life-long course of treatment.

Prosecutor: Do we know what causes someone with Ms. Ross' condition to kind of go downhill into that psychotic episode? Are there certain triggers that would cause that?

Forensic Psychologist 2: Well, yes and no. Certain factors can contribute to the likelihood or probability of having, for example, a manic episode with psychosis: Part of that involves a sleep schedule, and part of that involves participation in treatment to look for other triggers, it can involve being aware of manic symptoms in terms of an increased goal-directed activity, agitation. If the symptoms are seen approaching or increasing it would be important to jump back into treatment If it has been discontinued for some reason.

Prosecutor: Do symptoms of a psychotic episode always manifest themselves violently?

Forensic Psychologist 2: No.

Prosecutor: Okay. Is there an increased concern that someone violent through a psychotic episode in the past would be more likely to engage in violence during a psychotic episode in the future?

Forensic Psychologist 2: Yes, that would be a concern for a person doing a risk assessment of that individual: Based on how their psychotic episode in the past played out, there would be an increased risk for similar behavior moving forward.

Prosecutor: And is there any way to predict or guarantee whether or not somebody has a psychotic episode in the future?

Forensic Psychologist 2: Well, the best method of prediction is whether they are maintaining the course of treatment: If they stop the course of treatment by stopping medications, or engaging in substance use, or forget to or stop managing their sleep patterns, there's an increased risk.

Prosecutor: And there is still somewhat of a risk, or at least a risk that, even if they are doing those things, it is possible that they could have another psychotic episode.

Forensic Psychologist 2: Yes.

Prosecutor: And Doctor, as part of your evaluation, did you review the evaluation done by Forensic Psychologist 1?

Forensic Psychologist 2: Yes, I did.

Prosecutor: And in reviewing Forensic Psychologist 1's evaluation, were you in agreement with the things that Forensic Psychologist 1 had to say in his evaluation, or did you disagree with some of those things?

Forensic Psychologist 2: I believe that what I read in his report was consistent with what I saw in conducting my evaluation, and I don't recall any specific areas of dispute in terms of the facts of the case or applying those facts to the relevant questions of mental illness or appreciation of wrongfulness, for example; so, in general, I agree with the description provided by the Forensic Center examiner.

Prosecutor: And just lastly, during your -I think it was a three-hour in-person interview that you did, correct?

Forensic Psychologist 2: Yes.

Prosecutor: And during that interview what was Ms. Ross' demanor like?

Forensic Psychologist 2: Ms. Ross presented as anxious, somewhat withdrawn, and embarrassed about her behavior. She was organized and able to describe her history and function. She was cooperative and was not observed to be in any state of psychosis or agitation at the time that I met with her.

Prosecutor: Do you attribute that to her being medicated through Zyprexa and potentially Buspar?

Forensic Psychologist 2: I attribute it to the treatment with the medications certainly, but also there is a certain amount of structure in the jail environment: Sometimes it can exacerbate symptoms, but that also can help maintain stability.

Prosecutor: Thank you, Doctor. I don't have anything further.

Judge: Thank you, Doctor. You are excused.

Chapter 27: The Court's Ruling

Judge: Do you have any other witnesses?

Defense Council: I do not, your Honor.

Judge: Mr. Prosecutor, are there any rebuttal witnesses that the state intends to present?

Prosecutor: No, your Honor.

Judge: All right. Now, as we know, we're here over the last two days to determine whether or not Ms. Ross· not-guilty-by-reason-of-insanity pleas to all charges should be accepted by the court and it's the court's role to meld Michigan court Rule 6.302 with 6.304 when making its findings. Mr. Prosecutor, are there any closing statements you'd like to give at this time?

Prosecutor: Just briefly, your Honor. Your Honor, the court has sat here for the last day and a half and looked at the exhibits and listened to the testimony, and in some cases, listened to the exhibit. There isn't anything that I can say that would be more compelling than the chilling testimony in evidence that the court has seen and heard over these last few days. There's been ample evidence to prove that the defendant, Ms. Ross, murdered William Johnson and that she killed the two dogs willfully and without just cause: I think that's been presented very clearly, and during that entire incident, it's also clear that she possessed a firearm, based upon the testimony likely more than one given what was found at the scene. The statute and the case law require the firearm to be accessible and obtainable during the felony, she doesn't necessarily have to have it on her person the whole time, although I believe that during this, the evidence was she would have had it on her person. There's certainly one of the charges, Your Honor, is open murder, and there's been more than ample evidence of certainly Murder 2, but I also think that there is evidence of premeditation, specifically if the court looks to statements of "she had to finish him off," "beat him until he stopped moving", I think there was a statement of "beat him with things until he stopped moving then stabbed him" among other things.

Prosecutor: If the court looks at the testimony and the evidence, it appears there were multiple attempts by the defendant to kill Mr. Johnson, she wasn't successful at first, and when you look at the scene, it appears that this went on for some time, we don't know how long, but if the court looks to Mr. Johnson's home and the things like the furniture that's flipped over, many of those things appear to have been done during the struggle. Is it possible some of those things could have been done afterward? Yes. But for many of those things, including the broken lamps, there was evidence that, at one point, this started upstairs and ended downstairs. With all of those things, I certainly think that this court could make a finding that it has been shown that she committed first-degree murder, I think there's ample justification on the record for that. Either way, your Honor, the evidence and testimony do show that she murdered Mr. Johnson, that she killed both dogs without cause, and that she did indeed possess a firearm during these felonies. Now, as to her mental state, the evidence speaks basically for itself. The court has sat through much of the testimony. The testimony of the two different doctors was clear, as were some of the behaviors that were exhibited by the defendant during the course. Well, actually, the events leading up to this incident and also during the investigation by law enforcement. So, Your Honor, based upon everything, I would ask this court to make appropriate findings.

Judge: Thank you, Mr. Prosecutor. Ms. Defense Council?

Defense Council: I'll be brief as well, your Honor. We do not dispute that the evidence has clearly shown that Ms. Ross committed the crimes that she's charged with: I will leave it to the court's discretion to decide about the - whether it would be first-degree murder or whatever. I agree that some of the evidence could be looked at as revealing some level of premeditation, but it would also appear that, given the severity of her mental illness at the time, that she may not have been capable of such a thing. The evidence, as Mr. Prosecutor just pointed out, was compelling. Every single officer who testified indicated that it was clear to them that Ms. Ross was suffering from a severe mental illness at the time that she was interviewed by them just shortly after the killing of Mr. Johnson: Several of the officers indicated that in their 20-plus years of service, they have not seen anything more incredible than what they observed in this case. The court is aware that this is a plea-taking proceeding that requires the court to first determine that the acts were committed as charged, and, second, to determine that the defense has shown by a preponderance of the evidence that Ms. Ross was legally insane at the time.

Defense Council: We heard the doctors discuss the definition of insanity. MCL 768.21a indicates that an individual is legally insane if, as a result of mental illness, as defined in section 400 of the Mental Health Code, that person lacks substantial capacity either to appreciate the nature and quality or the wrongfulness of his or her conduct or to conform his or her conduct to the requirements of the law. The definition, in turn, of mental illness, is a substantial disorder of thought or mood that significantly impairs judgment, behavior, capacity to recognize reality, or ability to cope with the ordinary demands of life. And again, your Honor, the evidence that has been presented in this court has been compelling. It has shown by well over a preponderance of evidence, clear and convincing-plus evidence, that Ms. Ross was indeed mentally ill and legally insane at the time of these events. We would ask the court to accept her plea of not guilty because of insanity.

MY FATHER'S STORY

Judge: I would just like to begin and observe that we've had several people in the gallery, I suspect we have family and friends and people here supporting one side or the other, and you are all in my thoughts as we conclude this hearing. The findings that must be made following this hearing are, first, is there support that establishes that the defendant committed the acts charged; and second, has it been demonstrated by a preponderance of the evidence that the defendant was legally insane at the time of the offense? The court will return to the felony information and observe that the defendant is charged with six separate counts:

Judge: Count 1 is a charge of open murder: In Michigan, this is considered the short form of charging murder. The State has elected to charge this matter as open murder. If this were a jury trial, after evidence, a jury would have the opportunity to decide three options: Not guilty, first-degree murder, or second-degree murder and I'll discuss in a moment the elements of first-degree murder.

Judge: Count 2 alleges that this defendant committed the crime Of killing or torturing an animal in the third degree, a four-year felony, as does count 3, And counts 4, 5, and 6 all charge felony firearm. The elements of killing or torturing an animal in the third degree are that, without just cause, the defendant knowingly killed a dog, and the elements of felony firearm are as follows: That the defendant did carry or have in his or her possession a firearm, to with: A pistol at the time he or she committed or attempted to commit a felony, to with: Murder and animal cruelty in the third degree, and felony firearm charges are tied, specifically count 4 is tied to count 1, counts are tied to count 2, and count 6 is tied count 3 as required by Michigan law.

Judge: Now, turning to the jury instruction that sets forth the elements of first-degree premeditated murder, if this were a jury trial and I was tasked with instructing a jury, I would explain that the elements were as follows: First, that the defendant caused the death of, in this instance, William Johnson: That is, William Johnson died as a result of, in this instance, we have Medical Examiner 1's opinions as to the manner and cause of death: As I understand her opinion it includes both stabbing and blunt-force trauma: Second, that the defendant intended to kill William Johnson: Third, that this intent to kill was premeditated, that is, thought out beforehand: Fourth, that the killing was deliberate, which means the defendant considered to pros and cons of the killing, and thought about and chose her actions before she did it. There must have been real and substantial reflection for long enough to give a reasonable person a chance to think twice about the intent to kill: The law does not say how much time is needed, it is for you to decide, and that would be if I were instructing a jury, it would be for the jury to decide if enough time had passed under the circumstances of this case.

Judge: Finally, the killing was not justified, excused, or done under circumstances that reduce it to a lesser crime. Our composite jury instructions provide some guidance following the element section, and it's always been difficult, I think, to help jurors or lay people understand what the word "deliberate" and "premeditate" means in the context of the crime of murder.

Judge: The meaning of deliberate and premeditate has proved somewhat more elusive; however, Justice Levin's formulation in People versus Morrin, 31 Mich. APP, 301, a 1971 case that adopted People versus Vail, 393 Mich., 1975, noted that the following standard applies: "The ordinary meaning of terms will suffice. To premeditate is to think about it beforehand; to deliberate is to measure and evaluate the major facets of a choice or problem. As several courts have pointed out, premeditation and deliberation characterize a thought process undisturbed by hot blood. While the minimum time necessary to exercise this process is incapable of exact determination, the interval between initial thought and ultimate action should be long enough to afford a reasonable man time to subject the nature of his response or her response to a second look."

Judge: Now, returning to the first question before the court today, is there evidence that establishes support for finding that this defendant has committed the acts charged, one doesn't have to look beyond the defendant's own words to Trooper 4, Detective Trooper 1, Detective

Sergeant 1, Detective Sergeant 2 during separate interviews conducted by each of the police officers: This defendant acknowledged killing William Johnson.

Judge: Then, when you start to examine further how that killing was committed, it appears from the evidence she first attempted to use a handgun; that was unsuccessful. There was physical violence, there was bludgeoning with an instrument that caused the injuries that Medical Examiner 1 described finding to the head area of Mr. Johnson, and ultimately there were multiple stab wounds to Mr. Johnson's thoracic cavity and his stomach. Although there were, as I understood Medical Examiner 1's testimony, only seven openings, there were numerous wound paths within the body cavity that were discovered during the post-mortem investigation. So this was not a single gunshot, it wasn't a single stab, it wasn't a single bludgeoning, it was this display of rage over a period that ultimately appears to have led to Mr. Johnson's death, and if you apply what I've just read, the elements of first degree premeditated murder and the previous court's guidance as to how to determine whether this was a deliberate act or the act was premeditated, I'm satisfied that there is more than enough evidence before the court considering the investigation, Medical Examiner 1's testimony and, again, returning to the defendant's statements to the officers that there is sufficient support for finding that his defendant committed the crime of first degree premeditated murder.

Judge: There's also sufficient evidence for finding that she committed animal cruelty in the third degree, which was discovered at the scene by Trooper 3, and I believe it was Trooper 2 as well as Detective Sergeant 1, and then the crime lab that was there and discovered that the bodies of the dogs that had been stabbed, and when you couple that with the defendant's own words there's no justification for why these animals were killed, and there's, again, more than sufficient support for finding that she committed each count of animal cruelty.

Judge: And finally, when you look at the record and the weapons that were discovered, the gunshot hole that was discovered in the knee wall up in the bedroom area, the gunshot hole or what appears to be through a glass window and where the round was ultimately lodged in a branch as described by Trooper3, there's no question that during the midst of this criminal behavior by the defendant she carried or had in her possession a firearm, to with: A pistol and that pistol or pistols were accessible and under her control during the, in this court's opinion, the evidence shows during the premeditated murder of William Joseph Johnson, as well as the killing or torturing of each of the dogs; so, I'm satisfied that the first prong of Michigan Court Rule 6.304(C)(1) has been established sufficiently.

Judge: Now, turning to the second prong, to accept this defendant's not-guilty-by-reason-of-insanity pleas, the court must find that there's a preponderance of the evidence that demonstrates the defendant was legally insane at the time of the offense. Ms. Defense Council has read into the record the statutory definition of insanity; I'm going to do that again. Insanity is defined by our legislature at MCL 768.21a111 as follows: "It is an affirmative defense to a prosecution for a criminal offense that the defendant was legally insane when he or she committed the acts constituting the offense. An individual is legally insane if, as a result of mental illness or as a result of having an intellectual disability, that person lacks the substantial capacity either to appreciate the nature and quality or the wrongfulness of his or her conduct or to conform his or her conduct to the requirements of the law. Mental illness or having an intellectual disability does not otherwise constitute a defense of legal insanity."

Judge: And for those of you who are with us, the way an affirmative defense of insanity is raised, Michigan law requires notice to be given by a defendant that that is the defense they intend to raise at trial, and once that notice is made the court conducts hearing and an order enters in which a criminal defendant is then sent to the center for Forensic Psychiatry which is a division of the Michigan Department Of Health and Human Services for evaluation.

Judge: You've heard Forensic Psychologist 1's testimony today, and Forensic Psychologist 1 examined a court order. Historically, I'm not going to say in all cases, but before being elected to the bench, I was an assistant prosecutor for

13 years, but historically I think it's fair to say that attorneys, people that practice in criminal law, tend to view the center for Forensic Psychiatry as the state's expert; that's not always the case, but more often than not that's where the center aligns itself. There is case law that allows for, when a defendant disagrees with the center's examination and opinion, the defense can seek an independent evaluation, and that happens fairly commonly.

Judge: In this instance, the county Prosecutor, after reviewing Forensic Psychologist 1's report, has elected to seek out, really, a second independent evaluation, and you've also heard from Forensic Psychologist 2 who, although his opinion is slightly different, his conclusions are the same, and I'm going to read each of these into the record. I'm reading from page 14 of Forensic Psychologist 1's report that's been received by the court as Defendant's Exhibit F. Forensic Psychologist 1 concludes as follows: "As a result of her mental illness, it is my opinion Ms. Ross lacks substantial capacity to appreciate the nature and quality and the wrongfulness of her conduct at the time of the alleged offense."

Judge: "All collateral records, including the police report, 911 dispatchers, paramedics, and Munson Hospital, describe her behavior and demeanor as disorganized, bizarre, and delusional. Ms. Ross' account of the alleged incident at the time with police and hospital staff, as well as during this forensic evaluation, is consistent and suggests that she did not understand what was happening around her or the nature and quality of her actions. All of these records indicate Ms. Ross believed she had to kill Mr. Johnson to clean his soul and that she was being tested to be saved in the coming purge. She also believes several other bizarre delusions regarding space travel and the electric grid monitoring her house to stream a Facebook event through the government. To summarize, it is my opinion Ms. Ross was mentally ill at the time of the alleged offense, and it is also my opinion as a result of her mental illness Ms. Ross lacks substantial capacity to appreciate the nature and quality and the wrongfulness of her conduct. It is, therefore, my opinion she met the statutory requirements for a defense of legal insanity".

Judge: And then, turning to Forensic Psychologist 2's report, I'm going to read the entire paragraph into the record. "Dear Mr. Prosecutor, at your request, I have conducted an independent psychological evaluation of Angelee Ross regarding the issue of criminal responsibility. To complete this evaluation, the following procedures were conducted: Review of extensive discovery materials provided by the Prosecutor, including police reports, audio recordings, digital media, witness statements, and medical reports, review of reports issued by the Center for Forensic Psychiatry on July 23rd, 2021 and July 29th, 2021, review of available treatment records from Munson Health care Manistee, North Pines Health center, Manistee County Jail, Wellston Medical Center, Administration of Psychological

MY FATHER'S STORY

Testing, Personality Assessment Inventory, consultation with Mr. Prosecutor, and clinical interview with Ms. Ross.

Judge: The defendant was interviewed in person at the Manistee County Jail on January 21st, 2022, in a session lasting three hours. Following a thorough analysis of the available information, it is my opinion that Ms. Ross was mentally ill during the time in question: That is, she experienced psychotic symptoms in the form of hallucinations, paranoia, and delusions of reference that grossly impaired her contact with reality and guided her behavior. It is my opinion that the available information provides strong and consistent support for a finding of legal insanity.

Judge: Now, returning to the threshold necessary to accept the defendant's not guilty because of insanity plea, I explain that it requires by preponderance of the evidence. In Michigan, there are three standards of evidence: By a preponderance, clear and convincing, and beyond a reasonable doubt. A preponderance of the evidence has been described in our country as more likely than not, 51 percent versus 49 percent, it's the lowest standard of proof in our country, and I say that because I want those who are here to have some appreciation as to really what is required in this instance.

Judge: The court has more than just doctor's reports, however, we've heard the 911 call that Ms. Ross placed just days before this tragic killing of Mr. Johnson, and we've also heard her in her own words what she described experiencing and believing all of the police officers who had the opportunity to speak with her, and we've also heard her behavior after being arrested at the county jail, and what she was engaged in doing in her jail cell, we've also heard, for instance, that she was receiving messages from one of the animals or both of the animals. So, it's not simply the doctor's evaluations: We had the lay witness testimony, and we have the defendant's own words that I think we can all look to, and I'm certainly allowed to look to when deciding whether or not it's been demonstrated by a preponderance of the evidence the defendant was legally insane at the time of the offense, and given the record before me there's no other finding that I believe I can make then find that there has been a preponderance of the evidence presented that demonstrates this defendant was legally insane on March 17th, 2021 when she committed each of these crimes.

Judge: So, for that reason, as I explained to you, Ms. Ross, you understand that if I now accept your not-guilty-by-reason-of-insanity pleas again, I'm required to commit you to the Center for Forensic Psychiatry for up to 60 days, and then the center will prepare a report, and it's very possible, and I would suggest you should anticipate, that I will be ordered to direct or it will be recommended that I direct the Prosecuting Attorney to proceed in the probate court and pursue involuntary commitment proceedings in the probate court for Manistee county with regards to you, do you understand that?

Angelee: I understand that.

Judge: And that may result in your being hospitalized for the rest of your life, do you understand that as well?

Angelee: I understand.

Judge: And you're asking me to accept your pleas?

Angelee: I am.

Judge: And do you understand that if I accept your not-guilty-by-reason-of-insanity pleas, you don't have an automatic right to appeal, do you understand?

Angelee: I understand.

Judge: If you have a right to appeal, or if there's any basis to appeal, it's by application to the Michigan Court of Appeals, do you understand that?

Angelee: I understand that.

Judge: So, at this time, again, returning to 6.302 and 6.304, I find that the defendant's pleas of not guilty because of insanity have been properly supported as required by 6.304, that her pleas have been made knowingly, understandingly, voluntarily and accurately; the court will so accept her pleas. The court, at this time, will sign an order committing the defendant to the Center for Forensic Psychiatry for diagnostic examination for up to 60 days, following which the court will receive a report with instructions from the center as to how to proceed. The court also will be preparing a settled record that must be transmitted forthwith to the Center for Forensic Psychiatry. We have several exhibits. I'm happy to not only have our court reporter prepare the transcripts, which will be part of the settled record, and then include all of the exhibits that we've received in one packet to send to the Center for Forensic Psychiatry; there's no guarantee that those exhibits will be returned, do you understand that Mr. Prosecutor, Ms. Defense Council?

Prosecutor: I do, Your Honor.

Defense Council: Yes, Your Honor.

Judge: I'm also happy to keep these exhibits with the understanding that the parties submit identical copies that can be received by the court as part of the settled record and transmitted to the center so that we, as a court, maintain custody of the actual exhibits that have been received. I'll hear arguments, Mr. Prosecutor, how you'd like to proceed, and the reason I bring this up is I have not experienced this previously when we've had a not-guilty-by-reason-of-insanity plea where we've had, really, exhibits that are introduced. So, your thoughts?

Prosecutor: I guess, Your Honor, my thoughts would kind of depend on whether the center would be returning those exhibits: I believe that they would, but certainly if it would be better to make copies of those.

Judge: Typically, what would happen is that after a hearing, the exhibits would be returned to the parties because there's no longer a need for those exhibits at the trial court level. If you're more comfortable with me keeping those exhibits in the court file, then we need copies. If you're satisfied that the court should simply forward to the Center for Forensic Psychiatry your respective exhibits, Mr. Prosecutor, and your respective exhibits, Ms. Defense Council, that's what we'll do.

Defense Council: I have no objection to their being forwarded to the Forensic Center or Hospital, Your Honor, because we already have copies of the information, so I would leave it to the court's discretion and deter to Mr. Prosecutor's preference.

Prosecutor: We do have copies, Your Honor. As long as the center, I would think the center would be returning those exhibits as they're marked to the court, but certainly, I would be okay. I know that we certainly have copies of everything already.

Judge: All right. Then I will treat as part of the settled record that the court Rule and the statute require not only the transcript of the last two days that Mr. Court Reporter will be preparing in short order, but also all of the exhibits that have been received into evidence, and that entire packet will be forward to the center along with the order of commitment.

Defense Council: Yes, Your Honor.

Prosecutor: Very good.

Judge: Finally, Ms. Ross' bond is revoked. She'll remain in the custody of the Sheriff to await the demands of the center for Forensic Psychiatry: That may not be immediate, it depends on if they have a bed available, but they will notify the court, and I expect counsel when a bed is available and then she'll need to be transported to that location by the Manistee County Sheriff. If there's nothing further, that will conclude today's hearing.

Chapter 28: What Now?

And just like that, it was over... or so I thought. As I got up and walked out of the courtroom, I had a whirlwind of emotions. We had expected this outcome, but deep down, there was a part of me that wanted to hear the judge declare her guilty. Even though the judge acknowledged that the Prosecutor had presented enough evidence for all six felony charges, I still wasn't sure yet if that alone would bring me relief.

As we left the courtroom, we found ourselves in the hallway, where the Prosecutor, Detective Sergeant, and Detective Sergeant 2 joined us. They were discussing the verdict when the Defense Council approached our group. She wished us a safe journey home and hoped we could do some healing now that this was over. Then she came up to me and gave me a hug before leaving.

We started walking down the long hallway toward the elevators and the first floor, and the two detectives shook our hands and wished us well. Meanwhile, the Prosecutor and I lagged behind. I stopped him and said, "Mr. Prosecutor, my father would have been proud of you. You did an amazing job presenting the case." He was grateful for my words. He thanked me, we shook hands, and went our separate ways.

On July 23rd, 2022, we found ourselves once again sitting in the courtroom in Manistee, for the verdict of the 60-day mental health evaluation. The Center of Forensic Psychology had determined without a doubt that she was criminally insane and sentenced her to the mental health system. The Prosecutor then prepared an involuntary committal petition for her, which was submitted to probate court. Just 14 days later, we were sitting in a virtual Probate courtroom, where Angelee willingly consented to be committed to the mental health system.

There were virtual court hearings for a 60-day check-in, followed by another check-in after 90 days. The reports from the Forensic Center showed improvement in her condition. She was now able to take care of basic tasks like showering and changing her own clothes. She expressed she was happy to be there and had a genuine desire to figure out what was wrong with her.

According to the law, she is entitled to an annual probate hearing within the court system. During these hearings, her treatment and progress are discussed, including the possibility of transferring her to a less secure facility or even her release. Before anyone loses their mind that there is even a chance she could be released... Any discussion of her release would require the approval of multiple people. They would have to review the court transcripts, which you have now read in this book, and place their trust in her ability to never offend again.

MY FATHER'S STORY

Releasing her would also mean risking their own reputations. In my opinion, the chances of her ever being released from the mental health system are almost non-existent.

So, how does one end a book about the murder of their father? This question has haunted me since I started writing this book. I have rewritten this section countless times, searching for the perfect ending. In all the drafts, there was one constant, so I think I'll just end on that.

Pops wasn't big on social media, as he only had a Facebook account. The last thing he posted was a few weeks before he was murdered. I'll just let you reflect on it:

"On this road called life, you have to take good with bad, smile with the sad, love what you got, and remember what you had. Always forgive, but never forget, learn from your mistakes, but never forget. People change. Things go wrong. But just remember, the ride goes on."

The End

www.ingramcontent.com/pod-product-compliance
Lightning Source LLC
Chambersburg PA
CBHW070529010526
44118CB00012B/1076